❊ BUNGALOW ❊
BATHROOMS

Jane Powell

with photographs by Linda Svendsen

GIBBS·SMITH
P
PUBLISHER

Salt Lake City

First Edition
05 04 03 02 01   5 4 3 2 1

Published by
Gibbs Smith, Publisher
P.O. Box 667
Layton, Utah 84041

Orders: (1-800) 748-5439
www.gibbs-smith.com

Edited by Suzanne Taylor
Designed and produced by Woodland Studio
Printed and bound in China

Library of Congress Cataloging-in-Publication Data

Powell, Jane, 1952–
 Bungalow bathrooms / Jane Powell and Linda Svendsen.— 1st ed.
  p. cm.
 ISBN 1-58685-091-4
 1. Bathrooms—Remodeling. 2. Interior decoration. I. Svendsen,
Linda, 1954– II. Title.
 TH4816.3.B37 P68 2001
 643'.52'09730904—dc21
                    2001002897

Contents

Acknowledgments

THERE ARE MANY PEOPLE and organizations without whom this book would not have been possible. I would first like to thank Linda Svendsen for her beautiful photography and her willingness to take on bathrooms, which are extremely difficult to photograph. This might be a good place to mention that the wide-angle lenses needed to photograph a bathroom tend to distort the photo, making the rooms look much larger than they are in real life; where possible, I have included dimensions in the captions. So don't despair if your bathroom is tiny and the ones in the book all appear to be huge.

Next I would like to thank the homeowners who welcomed us into their houses and their bathrooms: Lorrie and Steven Bailey, Bret Bagne, Betty Balcom, Susan and Stephen Booth, Marilyn Citron and Kevin Flynn, Brian Coleman and Howard Cohen, Olivia Dresher, Meredith Emery, Gary Encinas and Bill Moore, Richard Fishman, Connie Garnett, Loretta and Gary Graham, Julie Hardgrove and Cliff Cline, Cathy Hitchcock and Steve Austin, Lani and Larry Johnson, Kelly Jones and Michael Murray, Sima Kahn and Alan Rothblatt, Sally and Louis Lewis, Manuel Lima, Marilyn Lundberg, Heidi Mollenhauer and Kirk Wise, Robert Noble, Joan and Don Nolte, Sue Rennie, Jeff Ross, Carrie Schnelker and Michael Sobieck, Sally Tobin and Andrew Jackson, Georgia and Harold Tolliver, Pierre Vedel, Vreni and Jerry Watt, Ron Webber and Bill Pfeifer, Calla Wiemer, Page Yarwood and Eli Koutchis, Chris York, and Tara Zucker. Thanks also to Jon Chaney and Larry Kreisman at Historic Seattle (Dearborn House), Teresa Wilkins and Lynda Guthrie at Dunsmuir House, Melissa Patton at the Lanterman House, Ted Bosley and Bobbi Mapstone at the Gamble House, Rick Knotts at the Riordan House, Dorothy Hubbard at the Stimson-Green Mansion, and Don Hooper at Vintage Plumbing.

We would never have found so many fabulous bathrooms without referrals from the following: Dianne Ayres and Tim Hansen at Arts and Crafts Period Textiles, Brian Coleman, Laurie Crogan, Riley Doty, Jane Friedrich, Loretta Graham, Sally and Louis Lewis, Christopher Molinar at the Gamble House Bookstore, Oakland Heritage Alliance, Pasadena Heritage, Mary Ellen Polson and Patricia Poore at *Old House Interiors*, Janelle Spatz, Laurie Taylor at Ivy Hill Interiors, and Cristi Walden.

Many people contributed knowledge, access to period books, catalogs and magazines, and websites, including Dianne Ayres and Tim Hansen, Riley Doty, Friederike Droegemueller, David Farr, and Mark Novakowski. I am especially grateful to Mark Novakowski for providing me with two period plumbing catalogs (courtesy of The Sink Factory), Riley Doty for information about tile, and Stephen Shaluta for additional photography.

The book would not be what it is without the fabulous illustrations by Betsy Martin, and I never would have finished on time without the invaluable organizational assistance of Valerie Fahnestock. I must also thank Jeanette Sayre for her assistance with the book proposal, her friendship, and her continuing advice on all matters aesthetic and otherwise. And I must thank my editor, Suzanne Taylor, who, as always, cleans up my words but leaves their spirit intact. I also acknowledge all at Gibbs Smith, Publisher, for their continuing support and enthusiasm.

In the fall of last year, shortly after beginning to write this book, I was diagnosed with Non-Hodgkins lymphoma, a cancer of the lymph system. After six months of chemotherapy, I am happy to report that I am in remission. That I was able to continue working on the book in the face of this can be attributed to both my innate stubbornness and need for distraction (to say chemotherapy is not fun would be rather an understatement), and also to the incredible support I received from my family, my friends, and even people I barely knew. Cancer is not a gift (I don't care what Bernie Siegel says), but what is a gift is the opportunity to find out how many lives you have touched, and that is amazing. I am particularly indebted to Jeannette Sherwin, who took it upon herself to send out e-mail updates about my condition to a list that soon grew to more than one hundred people. Without their support, I would not have been able to finish the book or the treatment. (Nor did people complain too much when I kept wanting to discuss toilets at dinner.)

I especially want to thank my parents, Nelson and Peg Powell, my two sisters, Mary Enderle and Nancy Klapak, my brother-in-law Rob Enderle (who built me a new computer), my niece, Karin Klapak, and my nephew, Brian Klapak (who designed my website). I learned from them that family doesn't just mean relatives, and I am grateful now more than ever to have an extended family of aunts, uncles, cousins, and friends. Their love and friendship is a constant in my life. Of course, my life would not be complete without my feline companions, Milo, Ubu, Emma, and Zoe. Emma and Ubu sat on my lap most of the time I was writing, and I would certainly not be in remission without the help of Feline Acupressure (a well-known complementary therapy).

Last but not least, I would like to dedicate this book to my grandparents, Ora and John William Powell, who did not get indoor plumbing till they moved into town in the 1950s.

Jane Powell
May 24, 2001

Introduction

An excellent plumber is infinitely more admirable than an incompetent philosopher. The society which scorns excellence in plumbing because plumbing is a humble activity, and tolerates shoddiness in philosophy because it is an exalted activity, will have neither good plumbing nor good philosophy. Neither its pipes nor its theories will hold water.

—John William Gardner

Only the cloud-lift pattern in the window sashes provides a hint that this all-white bathroom is in the 1908 Gamble House in Pasadena, California, by architects Charles and Henry Greene.

In many ways this book grew out of a discussion I began having a few years ago with my friend Tim Hansen, concerning whether there was such a thing as an Arts and Crafts bathroom. At the time I maintained that there really wasn't, that it would be nearly impossible to guess the architectural style of a house by looking at the bathroom. For instance, take a look at the back cover of this book. Without the art-glass door and distinctive woodwork, would there be any clue that this bathroom is in the Greene and Greene–designed Gamble House? After some research, I concluded that although there were bathrooms that showed design influence from the Arts and Crafts movement, this influence was mainly limited to décor, the manufacturers of fixtures being governed more by functional requirements. In the latter part of the nineteenth century, there were some bathrooms decorated in the prevailing Arts and Crafts or Aesthetic movement style, but in America during the heyday of the Arts and Crafts movement, the all-white sanitary bathroom prevailed. Even though colored tile came in the 1920s, bathrooms that "look" Arts and Crafts (mainly through the use of art tile) were mostly installed in the 1930s, long past the peak of the movement, and often in houses that were not Arts and Crafts in style.

These art-tile bathrooms differ significantly from a current trend that I would call "Arts and Crafts Revival." As manifested in bathrooms, this usually includes a fumed-oak vanity with hammered-copper pulls, lots of fumed-oak woodwork, stained glass, art tile, and other stylistic hallmarks of the Arts and Crafts period, often combined with more contemporary elements. While this may be a legitimate thing to do in a new house, in an old house, it just screams "turn of the twenty-first century."

In a way, the title *Bungalow Bathrooms* is a misnomer. These bathrooms were found in all kinds of late-nineteenth and early-twentieth-century houses: Italianate, Queen Anne, Second Empire, Gothic Revival, Stick, Colonial Revival, Foursquare, Georgian, Shingle, Arts and Crafts, Bungalow, Prairie, Tudor, Provincial, Spanish Colonial, Mediterranean, Mission Revival, Art Deco and Modern, early Ranch houses, and any other kind of house from about 1870 to 1950, not to mention apartment buildings from these eras.

This isn't really a "how-to" book; it's more of a "what-to" book. What there was, when it was available, how it got that way, how it went together, and how to solve various problems are all covered. Obsessive restoration and compromise solutions are explored for each element, allowing you to pick and choose among various options.

A period bathroom will simplify your life. Whether you are restoring an old one or building a new one, the range of appropriate fixtures, hardware, and other elements is limited compared to today's contemporary choices. This means far fewer decisions to make, though this is not to say there aren't still a lot of decisions. I encourage you to read other books and magazines about bathroom design and remodeling to get a working knowledge of the basic concepts, available materials, contractors and contracts, code requirements, and other things you will need to know when redoing a bathroom.

As Linda and I looked for bathrooms to photograph for this book, we were surprised at how many completely intact historic bathrooms we found. This puzzled me, since the bathroom is the second most likely room to have been remodeled in an old house, after the kitchen. I have come to the conclusion that there are two reasons for this: first, bathroom technology was mostly perfected in the nineteenth century and has changed very little since then, so these bathrooms are still functional for twenty-first-century life; second, it's just too much trouble to rip out all the tile—tile on a mortar bed lasts pretty much forever, and it's hard to demolish.

It is true that as our expectations of bathrooms increased during the latter part of the twentieth century, many perfectly functional bathrooms were ripped out or "modernized," replaced with the latest trendy designs of a particular decade, with the encouragement of various people who stood to make money from the endeavor. Original bathrooms were rarely documented, and they have not been protected other than by caring homeowners. Yet they are an important piece of history, one that has had far more impact than wars, politics, or any of the other things that history books usually concern themselves with. Few would argue that indoor plumbing and all that goes with it is the basis of modern civilization. Indeed, anyone who has ever visited a Third World country or gone backpacking has probably come home with a better appreciation of his or her own bathroom.

Historic bathrooms can easily be made to function for the twenty-first century without compromising their integrity. The craftsmanship, as well as the now-irreplaceable resources that went into them, should not be lightly discarded. Even a modest house was built with old-growth lumber of a quality that is no longer readily available, and we can't afford to send those sorts of resources to the landfill just because we want to be fashionable.

As a society, we have become remarkably self-centered, and we are no longer able to distinguish between "want" and "need." If you are in a wheelchair, then possibly you "need" to replace your bathtub with a roll-in shower. But you don't "need" a fireplace in your bathroom, and just because you may "want" one, that is no reason to rip out a historic bathroom. If your house is old, you are not the first owner, and you will not be the last. We are only temporary caretakers of these houses and should not do anything that some subsequent owner will be cursing us for, as we may now be cursing whoever painted all the natural woodwork or put in that horrible 1970s kitchen. Before you do anything, consider what it will look like to someone seventy-five years from now—will it cause them to remark sarcastically, "Oh, look, tumbled marble and a vessel sink, how very turn-of-the-century"? A bathroom that is remodeled to be stylish for whatever decade it's remodeled in will eventually look dated. A bathroom that is appropriate to the period of the house, on the other hand, appears timeless. It belongs there.

There is no better time than right now to restore or re-create a period bathroom. Appropriate elements are available as never before, at the mass-market level as well as the high-end. Retro styling in fixtures, lighting, cabinets, tile, faucets, and hardware is currently trendy. It's never been easier to find what you need for a historic bathroom.

"Don't reinvent the wheel— steal the whole car!"

Catherine Horsey

People began asking me to write this book even before I had finished *Bungalow Kitchens*. As with kitchens, although there was information available on historic bathrooms, it had never been assembled in one place. There was also a lot of misinformation. I hope this book will rectify that, and I also hope it will convince you to honor the past by restoring or re-creating a period bathroom in your home.

One final warning: this book contains puns. If you object to puns, ignore them. I like puns, it's my book, and I get to put them in.

—Jane Powell

History of the Modern Bathroom

"*T*elevision is like the invention of indoor plumbing. It didn't change people's habits. It just kept them inside the house."

~Alfred Hitchcock

Claustrophobic but functional, a ring shower over a Roman pedestal tub is the centerpiece of a subway-tiled bathroom in the 1911 Lanterman House in La Cañada-Flintridge, California. A hand-painted mural of irises decorates the frieze above the tile wainscot.

The evolution of the modern bathroom is neither linear nor orderly. But parts of it are pretty disgusting, so don't read this chapter over lunch. Some ancient civilizations had bathrooms that were far more "modern" than the average bathroom of the mid-nineteenth century. Indeed, a twentieth-century Englishman was heard to complain of his Oxford college that it "denied him the everyday sanitary conveniences of Minoan Crete." And he was not far off—a bathroom (circa 1700 B.C.) unearthed at Knossos contains a water-flushed latrine, a basin with running water, and a highly decorated tub little different from those commonly featured in late-nineteenth-century plumbing catalogs. Recently, Chinese archeologists unearthed a two-thousand-year-old toilet with running water, a stone seat, and comfortable armrests in the tomb of a king of the western Han Dynasty (he evidently wanted to take his throne with him). The Romans elevated bathing to an art form, and some parts of their plumbing technology are in use to this day; yet with the fall of the Roman Empire, that knowledge was lost and was not fully rediscovered until the nineteenth century. What followed was the Dark Ages, in more ways than one.

Early humans seem to have lived by the waterside, since water was needed and there was no way to carry it very far. Eventually someone would have noticed that water could be useful for more than drinking, and would have made of the river or brook a "convenience" for carrying away excrement. Eventually someone else would figure out that it was best to drink upstream of the "convenience," and thus sanitary planning was born.

A few thousand years later, the idea that natural elements such as water represented powers greater than man led to sound sanitary taboos based on magic or religion. It was easier to make the water supply sacred and warn that interference with it could arouse divine wrath than explain why it should not be tampered with. As tribes moved away from the river in search of better hunting grounds, and water had to be carried, it became more precious. Bathing would have been rare. Until a civilization was advanced enough to have either slaves or water pipes, it just wasn't worth the trouble to bathe at home. And rather than progressively evolving from some sort of crude stone tub, the bath emerges already well developed when civilization is ready for it. Since pottery was already established as a craft, and a bathtub is nothing more than a very large dish, no new technology had to be invented, except for ways of handling a dish of that size. All that was needed was a customer with access to adequate labor who also cared for the delights of home bathing, i.e., a king.

CONCRETE EVIDENCE

The first known bath was built on Crete for King Minos some 3,600 years ago. The terra-cotta tub is startling because it is almost identical in form to freestanding tubs of today, set in an elegantly decorated bathroom with efficient plumbing. In the ancient cities of the Indus Valley, which flourished from 2500

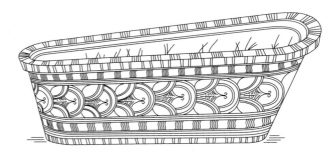

Ancient tub

to 1500 B.C., many houses had bathrooms and water-flushed latrines, which drained into brick-lined pits with outlets near the top (rather like modern septic tanks) that led to street drains. The ancient Egyptians (at least the wealthy ones) used human-powered showers, standing on a limestone slab while the servants poured water over them. Though they were early developers of piping and metalwork, they used earth closets rather than water-flushed latrines. The ancient Greeks also bathed at home, heating water in a three-legged bowl by the fire, and then carrying it to the bathhouse to be diluted with cold water in a metal tub to the proper temperature. Brief, cold baths or showers were also an adjunct to the Greek gymnasium. And many Greek houses were equipped with closets or latrines that drained into a sewer beneath the street, apparently using wastewater for flushing. But it was the Romans who truly elevated bathing (and plumbing) to an art form.

ROMAN AROUND

The public baths were the focus of Roman communal life, and the highest technical and architectural skills were devoted to building them. The baths of Caracalla covered an area of 121,000 square feet, and the baths of Diocletian were said to have been twice that large. Rome was supplied with water by thirteen aqueducts, and at its peak used 300 gallons per person per day (in our time, the approximate usage for a family of four). In the fourth century A.D., Rome had 11 public baths and 856 private baths. As well as private water-flushed latrines, there were also public ones: Rome had 144 as of A.D. 315. And if you think graffiti in public restrooms is a recent problem, consider this graffiti found in Herculaneum, one of the cities buried in lava and ash by the eruption of Mount Vesuvius in A.D. 79: APOLLONIVS MEDICVS TITI IMP. HIC CACARIT BENE translates as "Apollonius, physician of Emperor Titus, had a good crap here." Or this, found in a public bath in Pompeii, "Wine, women, and the baths destroy our bodies and our minds, but make life worth living." The public baths opened at about one o'clock in the afternoon. One could warm up with a game of tennis, follow with some moderate sweating in the *tepidarium*, then undress and be anointed with oils and ointments. Next, one would move onto the *calidarium* (rather like a sauna) to sweat more, then briefly into the *laconicum*, a hot spot directly over the furnace. There, warm, tepid, and then cold water would be poured over one, followed by scraping with a *strigil* (a curved metal tool with a groove to collect the excess water), and then sponging and re-anointing. Finally, one would take a plunge in the *frigidarium* (cold bath) before strolling around to meet friends.

The Romans built baths wherever they went, using local hot springs if they were available, such as those at Bath in England. Much of their plumbing technology is still in use (the word *plumbing* comes from the Latin *plumbum*, meaning "lead"). They used fired earthenware as well as lead pipes, and had such modern conveniences as radiant-floor heating, showers, and water piped into kitchens and laundry rooms. Of course, they may also have had a high incidence of lead poisoning. After the fall of the Roman Empire, it took centuries for plumbing to return to that level of sophistication.

GARGOYLE WITH SALT WATER

The barbarian tribes used primitive latrines or the great outdoors. An excavation of a Viking settlement in York, England, uncovered a thousand-year-old piece of excrement, affectionately known as the "Lloyd's Bank Turd" (after its location beneath Lloyd's Bank). It is insured for $34,000.

During the Dark Ages, the monasteries were the main bastions of cleanliness, although the custom of washing one's hands before meals was maintained because people were still eating with their hands, flatware not having come into general use. Some monasteries had running water in lead or wooden pipes, and some even had water-flushed latrines, usually accomplished by diverting a stream. (Though people were aware of the problem, apparently no one did much about separating drinking water from sewage until well into the nineteenth century.) Bathing, when it was done, was done in wooden tubs that had to be filled and emptied by hand. Due to the difficulty of procuring enough hot water, bathing was usually communal, with the whole family and any guests sharing the tub while the water was hot. Soap was (re)invented in the fourteenth century, and was usually scented with herbs or rose petals, but its use was far from general.

Public baths, or "stews," forgotten since the Roman occupation, came back into favor as the returning Crusaders taught the merits of "the Turkish bath." But within a century they had died out again, due to the spread of plague and other infections, and

Garderobe outlet

because of church objections to immoral business (prostitution) carried out on the side. Most were closed down during the reign of Henry VIII, and the remaining few were strictly regulated.

Westminster Palace was the first private house in the British Isles to have an underground drainage system, having had a water supply installed by Henry III in 1233. Henry was apparently way ahead of his time sanitation-wise. He built privies in all his palaces, and even went so far as to insist on having them built in houses he was visiting. For the rest of the populace, however, it was cesspits and chamber pots, the contents of which were simply dumped out the window into the street. It was common courtesy to warn the pedestrians below with the French phrase *"gardez l'eau"* ("look out for the water"), which led to the British slang term for toilet, *loo*. The cesspits had to be cleaned at intervals, and the *gongfermors* whose job it was were paid handsomely (forty shillings, or about two pounds—a lot of money in those days). Most of the palace privies, as well as the public latrines, were simply cantilevered out from the walls so that the contents dropped directly into a stream or moat, or in some cases, onto the ground. At Beaumaris in Wales, the filth was expelled through grimacing stone faces, no doubt installed by a builder with a sense of humor.

As early as the medieval period, the English were already referring to the privy (from the Latin *privatus*, meaning "apart, secret, not publicly known") by various euphemisms such as "necessary house" (a term still in use in America in the nineteenth century), or "garderobe" (wardrobe). It is interesting to note that in *The Life of St. Gregory* the privy was recommended for "uninterrupted reading." Actually, the privy was usually in a room off the garderobe, with a right-angled passage leading to it to waylay the wafting odors. Some believed that the stench from the privy kept bugs out of the clothes stored in the wardrobe. The later alternative to the privy was the close stool, basically a box

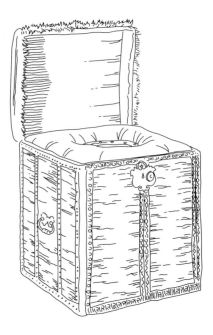

Close stool

containing a chamber pot with an appropriately sized hole in the lid. Some of the royal ones were quite elaborate, covered in padded velvet and studded with gilt nails, although this didn't really disguise the fact that they were disgusting. All this nastiness could have come to an end as early as 1596, when Sir John Harington, a godson of Queen Elizabeth I, invented a valve water closet. Though not resembling a modern toilet in form, the technology was similar to some nineteenth-century toilets that were precursors of the toilet as we know it. He installed one at his own house in Kelston, near Bath, and another for his godmother in Richmond Palace, though apparently she preferred her close stool. Evidently these were the only two ever installed. Sir John was 250 years ahead of his time, and his only reward is the use of his name as a slang word for toilet.

Exceptions to the general lack of bathing were the various hot springs, such as those at Bath, which had been in continuous use, not so much for cleanliness but because they were believed to be healing. This had more to do with religion than medicine. Indeed, many of these hot springs are still used today, and spas and resorts have sprung up around them.

By the sixteenth century, showers had made an appearance. In 1581, Michel de Montaigne gave this account of his stay at a villa in Italy:

There is water to drink here and to bathe in: a covered bath, vaulted and rather dark, half as wide as my dining room in Montaigne. There is also a certain dripping apparatus they call la doccia (the shower): this consists of pipes by which you receive hot water on various parts of the body, and especially on the head, the water coming down on you in steady streams and warming the part of your body that they are beating down on: and then the water is received in a wooden trough, like that of washerwomen, along which it flows away.

Showers were probably not very common at this time, not really reaching their full flowering until the twentieth century.

SUN KING TUB

By the seventeenth century, organized sanitation was slowly improving, and efforts were being made to channel water more efficiently into towns and cities. Reservoirs were built at high points, allowing gravity-fed water to flow into the city. With increased availability of water, a simple version of the water closet appeared. Although slightly less primitive than Sir John Harington's invention, it was basically just a marble bowl with a plug that, when pulled, allowed the contents to fall into a D-shaped, water-filled trap with a pipe at the top. It didn't work very well but continued a line of inventions, developments, and improvements that eventually led to the modern toilet. Even so, water closets were not widespread, even among the wealthy, and most continued to depend on privies and chamber pots.

The popular belief that seventeenth-century nobles, while dressed in silks and laces, used large quantities of perfume to mask the fact that they rarely bathed is not entirely true. The palace at Versailles had more than a hundred bathrooms during the reign of Louis XIV, though they were later dismantled. Marie Antoinette bathed daily, using one bath for washing and another for rinsing (not unlike a two-bowl kitchen sink). However, the close stool continued to be used, and indeed, was given an official role and treated as a throne at which audiences could be granted. It was considered a great privilege (by some, anyway) to be granted such an audience.

Developments in the water closet continued in the eighteenth century, but whether these developments could be characterized as "improvements" is questionable. Still, author Jonathan Swift had two water closets installed in 1729, which he dramatized in a poem:

Two temples of Magnifick Size,

Attract the curious Trav'llers Eyes,

That might be envied by the Greeks,

Rais'd up by you in twenty weeks;

Here, gentle goddess Cloacine

Receives all Off'rings at her shrine,

In Sep'rate cells the He's and She's,

Here pay their vows with bended knees:

For, 'tis prophane when sexes mingle

And ev'ry Nymph must enter single;

And when she feels an inward motion,

Comes fill'd with Rev'rence and Devotion.

The bashful Maid, to hide her Blush;

Shall creep no more behind a Bush;

Here unobserv'd, she boldly goes,

As who would say, to Pluck a Rose.

ROUNDS OF THE NIGHT TABLE

Gradually the close stool lost its place of honor, and began to be hidden away in another piece of furniture or disguised as something else, such as a pile of books. In the eighteenth century, gentlemen had even managed to get the chamber pot into the dining room for their relief, and the billiard room and the smoking room as well, where it was hidden behind shutters or curtains or disguised as a piece of furniture. All of these pots had to be paraded through the house at some point for emptying, to be collected by the "night

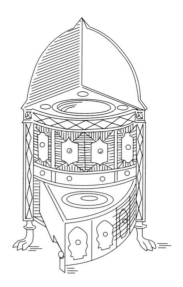

Sheraton Basin

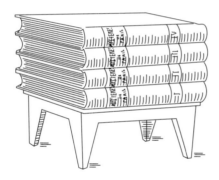

Book Toilet

soil men." This trade was as elegantly advertised as it was inelegant, featuring cards emblazoned with flamboyant script and romantic nocturnal scenes, all surrounded by swags of roses and such.

As the chamber pot began to be disguised in a piece of furniture (in a "night table" or "commode"—technically any decorative piece with drawers, but also still a euphemism for toilet—or in a "shaving table," which contained a place for the chamber pot), some now-famous furniture makers such as Chippendale, Sheraton, and Hepplewhite got in on the act. Sheraton advised that the "lodging room" should

include such pieces as were necessary for "the accidental occasions of the night."

Another eighteenth-century invention was the bidet, which can only be described with any delicacy as a device for cleansing the "nether regions" or perhaps the Monty Pythonesque "naughty parts." It was first mentioned in 1710 by the Marquis d'Argenson, who was charmed to be granted an audience by Mademoiselle De Prie while she sat. It was advertised in Paris, but one early dealer seemed to be unclear on what it was, offering it as "a porcelain violin case with four legs." This suggests the original shape was more of a figure eight, likely a better fit than the modern shape. Madame Pompadour owned two; one cased in rosewood with floral inlay, the other of walnut with a backrest and gilt nails. Much misinformation has caused this innocent fixture to become associated primarily with post-coital cleansing, and therefore to be viewed as somewhat illicit. A similar thing has happened to the word *douche*, which is simply the French word for shower.

The chilliness of a marble bath, as well as its weight and cost, led to a search for lighter-weight

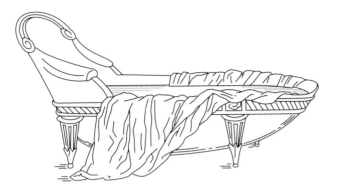

Demi Bain

bathtub materials. It was usual to line a wooden bath with copper or lead—copper being the most popular, as it was malleable and didn't rust, but it was also expensive. Tin was sometimes used as well. Sheet iron rusted, and the casting of an iron bath was beyond the technology of the time. Most baths of the eighteenth century greatly resembled furniture and were either made like chaise lounges or sofas, with padded backs and the fine woodworking of the cabinet-maker all about.

FLUSH WITH PRIDE

Tinkering with the water closet continued through the late eighteenth and into the nineteenth century, and produced some truly horrifying contraptions, although eventually the modern siphon-jet toilet (which we still use) was perfected. In the pan closet, for instance, a hinged metal pan kept a few inches of water at the bottom of an upper bowl until a handle was pulled. This was supposed to swing the pan down, tipping the contents into a cast-iron or lead receiver and thence into a trap below. Unfortunately, the contents generally got stuck in the receiver instead of going into the trap. In spite of this flaw, these closets were still being produced as late as 1891.

The even worse "hopper" closet, a simple cone-shaped vessel that went straight down to the trap, followed this. It had too much surface area to be properly cleaned by the trickle of water provided. S. Stephens Hellyer, a sanitarian of the day, suggested that hoppers could be put to a better purpose, "used by market gardeners to protect rhubarb from frost." Nonetheless, they were still being produced as late as 1926.

In 1775, Alexander Cummings, a watch and clock

Hopper closet

maker, took out a patent for a new type of water closet with an important feature, the S-trap, which had never been seen before. In 1778, this invention was again altered and nearly perfected by Joseph Bramah. Bramah was a cabinetmaker by trade who, in his spare time, also managed to invent the hydraulic press, rotary engines, steam engines, pens, printing machines, and locks. He improved on Cummings's sliding valve by replacing it with a flap valve, which was so successful that thousands of later copies (and a few originals) are still in use in Britain today.

In 1860, Reverend Moule patented an "Earth Closet," based on the idea that sifted dry earth or sand were excellent deodorizers, and that the resulting product could be used as fertilizer. A cone behind the seat was filled with earth or sand to be released down a chute when the handle was pulled. In reality, for deodorizing this worked about as well as it does in a cat box.

About 1870 came the "wash-out" closet: an all-earthenware closet in which a shallow bowl holds an inch or so of water. The flush empties the bowl but loses most of its force in doing so, and, says Hellyer, "gravitates through the trap in a most unselfish kind of way, taking little or nothing with it." In spite of this, Thomas Twyford sold hundreds of thousands in Britain between 1881 and 1889. In 1883, he introduced the pedestal version, called the "Unitas," which had an oak tree in raised relief on the bowl. "Unlike ordinary W. C. basins, it is not enclosed with woodwork," his catalogue proclaimed, "but is fully exposed, so no filth nor anything causing offensive smells can accumulate or escape detection."

The "Siphonic Closet" of J. R. Mann also dates from about 1870. In this closet, a fast flush was followed by a slower after-flush, while syphonic action kept things swirling.

George Jennings's "Pedestal Vase" won the Gold Medal Award at the Health Exhibition of 1884, hav-

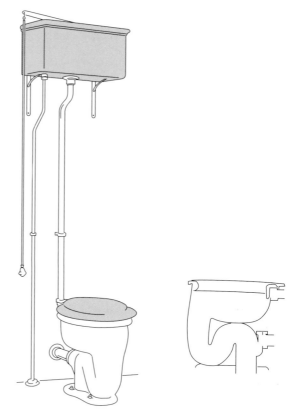

Wash-out closet

ing completely cleared the following items with a two-gallon flush: "10 apples averaging 1 1/4 inches in diameter, 1 flat sponge about 4 1/2 inches in diameter, and 4 pieces of paper adhering closely to the soiled surface." In 1884, the firm of Humpherson and Company patented the first "Wash-down closet," the Beaufort. It should be mentioned that all of these closets required a tank or cistern, usually placed high on the wall above the bowl, although a few low-tank toilets were offered as well. The high tanks allowed gravity to increase the velocity of the flush. Initially tanks were made of wood with a copper or lead lining—these were later replaced by vitreous china tanks.

Humpherson's professional rival was the now-

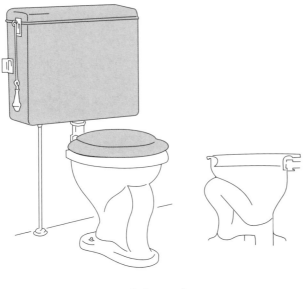

Wash-down toilet

Embossed floral designs decorate the bowl of a wash-down toilet at the 1904 Riordan House in Flagstaff, Arizona. It sits on a battleship linoleum floor.

legendary Thomas Crapper, who, contrary to popular belief, was not the inventor of the toilet. His main interest lay more in cisterns and water-waste preventers. Of the nine patents held by Crapper, only three were for water closets, and the most famous product attributed to him, the "Silent Valveless Water Waste Preventer," was actually patented by a Mr. Albert Giblin. (It is possible that Crapper bought the patent rights in order to market the device himself, since he advertised it.) The Metropolitan Water Act of 1870 required water-waste preventers to be built into water-closet tanks, and indeed, many high-tank toilets of the nineteenth century used only two gallons of water per flush. He did serve as the royal sanitary engineer for many members of England's royalty, overseeing the installation of all the drains and sanitary fittings at Sandringham, but he was never knighted. American soldiers passing through England during World War I and seeing toilets emblazoned "T. Crapper" coined the slang term *crapper*. It is unrelated to the word *crap*, which has

several definitions, according to the *Oxford English Dictionary*, including husk of grain or chaff, dregs of beer or ale, and excrement or defecation. It was first used in the latter way in 1846.

The British firms above, and many others, produced hundreds of variations on the water-closet theme during the nineteenth century, including

Lion Toilet

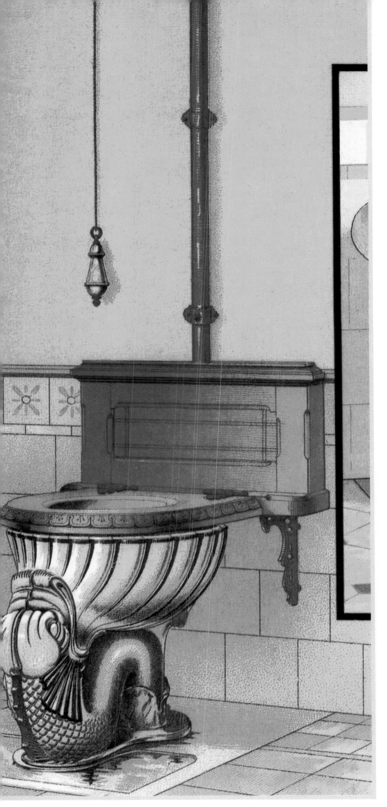

Dolphin toilet

"Trapless Twin Basin" closets, "Ventilating Pan" closets, as well as "Treadle Action" and "Pneumatic Combinations." There was the "Elastic Valve," "Flusherette Valve," "Pan Valve," "Valve Hopper," "Trapless Valve," not to mention the mysterious "Water Battery," and the closet with "Self-Acting Seat." Names were an important aspect of the marketing of water closets, with names like "Deluge," "Maelstrom," and "Niagara" suggesting a strong flushing action, or names such as "Adamant" conveying durability. And besides the technology, there was art: bowls were cast in the shapes of lions, dolphins, swans, architectural columns, etcetera; the outsides of bowls were covered with raised and/or hand-painted decoration, the inside of the bowl could also be decorated. Tanks and cisterns got the same treatment. These were the most beautiful toilets ever produced. All were advertised with the florid prose of the era in full-color catalogues.

Plumb Crazy

Meanwhile, in America, a similar progression was taking place, starting with pan closets in the 1830s and progressing to hopper and plunger closets. There were also proponents of Reverend Moule's earth closet, including Catherine Beecher and her sister, Harriet Beecher Stowe, who wrote in *The American Woman's Home*, "The earth closet is an invention which relieves the most disagreeable item in domestic labor, and prevents the disagreeable and unhealthful effluvium which is almost inevitable in all family residences." They were, of course, wrong. We were running somewhat behind Britain in the sanitary department, and many "sanitary appliances," as they were called, were imported from England until the late nineteenth century, when we finally caught up. Partly this was due to the craftspeople of the English pottery industry, who were already skilled at making washbasins and toilet bowls, which require a very different clay body from vases and such.

Starting about 1873, Thomas Maddock, who had been trained in china decorating in Staffordshire, began to produce basins and toilet bowls for a Trenton, New Jersey, firm. His early attempts had less than a 10-percent success rate, but he kept at it and eventually figured it out. He also found a way to incorporate a brass fitting (called a spud) on the bowl for connecting it to the tank, a connection that had previously been jury-rigged. New variations of water closets continued to be patented, and, given the American fascination with gadgetry, some of the devices were quite complex, which, of course, caused them to break down constantly. They weren't very attractive either, so most were encased in wood.

By the 1870s we had mostly caught up with Britain, and in 1876, William Smith of San Francisco was issued the first patent for a siphon-jet water closet, the type we still use.

In 1877, Charles Harrison of New York patented the oval bowl so common today. In round bowls, centrifugal force could cause the incoming water to flow upward, so a drip tray (referred to as a "save-all tray") was standard equipment. The shape of an oval bowl broke up the centrifugal force, so the tray was no longer necessary. Wash-out and wash-down closets also continued to be manufactured, however, well into the twentieth century.

Bathtubs had continued to be made of sheet metal, as they were in the eighteenth century, usually encased in wooden boxes or wainscoting. Copper, tin, lead, zinc, or iron was commonly used. Often there was a seam at the bottom, which tended to open up over time and cause leakage. The insides of the tubs were often painted, and the paint was not very durable. Because of these defects, American manufacturers began to experiment with cast-iron tubs (as

well as toilets and washbasins). One of the first was Mott Iron Works, which was selling tubs as early as 1866. In 1873, it was the first to produce cast-iron tubs with porcelain enamel—rather than painted—finishes on the inside. The outsides continued to be painted, usually quite elaborately. Early enamel finishes were somewhat less than satisfactory, consisting of a porous base coat, with a surface coat that was mixed with alcohol and floated onto the piece. The porous base coat allowed rust to form and discolored the top coat. In the early 1880s, the Standard Sanitary Manufacturing Company began to experiment with a new process that used "dredging," whereby the vitreous top glaze was sifted onto the piece before firing. This gave a superior finish and is still the method used today.

Other manufacturers took a different approach, and went to all-clay "porcelain" bathtubs. (A note about porcelain: it is technically a ceramic body or clay consisting of kaolin, quartz, and feldspar, which, when fired, produces ceramic ware that is hard, translucent, and nonporous. This term was thrown around with great abandon in the nineteenth century, and continues to be abused to this day.) Originally these could only be imported from England at great cost, but the Trenton Fireclay and Porcelain Company, which previously had produced firebricks, began to experiment with "porcelain" sanitary ware made of fireclay, with a slip of china (slip is basically liquefied clay) and a top glaze. By the 1890s, Mott Iron Works was buying all of their production, and in 1902 the two companies merged. By the late nineteenth century, the tub interior had taken on the familiar shape we still use: slanted at the back, straight at the front. Most were footed, with the familiar ball-and-claw foot being the most common, though criticism of the housekeeping problems posed by footed tubs was already beginning to be heard.

SITZ AROUND THE HOUSE

Much of the bathing in the nineteenth century had little to do with cleanliness. Instead, it had to do with health. There was widespread belief that water could cure all kinds of ills, either by drinking it or being immersed in it in various ways. (That we still somewhat believe this is why there are spas and bottled mineral water.) Hydropathy was big business. There were all kinds of baths: the sponge bath, the lounge bath, the sitz bath, the hip bath, the shower bath, the vapor bath, etc. Dr. John Bell, a Philadelphia practitioner, gave this description of a sitz bath: "Dipping Sitz is a term applied to dipping the posterior part of the body a dozen or more times in cold water. This should be done slowly, and followed with friction. It is highly beneficial in cases of nervous debility or a relaxed condition of the generative parts." There was great enthusiasm for cold water and cold showers, but this began to die out as hot water became more readily available. Those who tried to connect bathing to cleanliness faced an uphill battle early in the century. A popular 1837 etiquette book, *The Young Lady's Friend*, with uncharacteristic bluntness, advised that "no one can be quite certain of never offending any one's delicate olfactory nerves, whose arm-pits are not subjected to a thorough washing with soap and water every day." But it was not until the end of the century that bathing and cleanliness really became connected.

As bathtubs progressed, showers began to be more common. Early showers were simply a water tank on legs over some sort of receptacle, often just a hip or sitz bath rather than a full tub. The shower (usually cold) was operated by pulling a chain or lever to release the water. The tanks generally weren't very big, because the shower was of short duration. This method was followed by the hooded bath, with the shower built into one end of the tub under a protec-

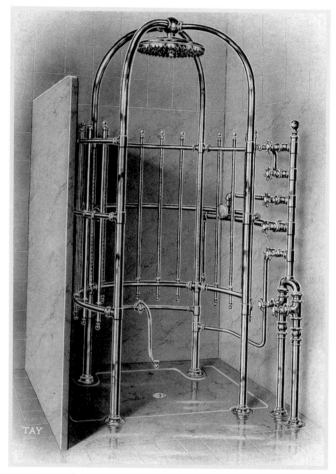

A symphony of nickel-plated pipes and valves distinguishes this cage shower set into a marble stall.

tive hood. Some of these contained very simple showers similar to modern ones, while others contained elaborate pipes and nozzles producing something more akin to an aquatic amusement park ride, with names like "Douche," "Spray," "Jet," "Sitz," "Wave," and "Plunge." Originally paneled in wood, later versions used painted sheet metal. During the same time period, simpler "cage" showers consisting of a metal ring with a cylindrical waterproof curtain and piping were also produced. These could either be fitted over a tub or stand separately over a shallow "receiver" of china, cast iron, or marble. They were simpler only in the sense that they didn't have a hood—many had the same elaborate variety of sprays as their hooded counterparts.

A hand-painted china basin set underneath a gracefully shaped marble slab features an unusual visible drain. Sinks like this would have been set on top of cabinets, or hung on decorative wall brackets. (Courtesy of Vintage Plumbing.)

The simple washstands and commodes of the eighteenth century gave way to a new larger washstand around 1830. More like a table than a stand, it had a backsplash and shelf above, a marble top, and a shelf for a china slop-pail below. Many also included towel bars and mirrors. There was room for a larger washbowl and jug, as well as soap dishes and other accoutrements. When running water arrived later in the century, the previously portable bowl became a fixture sunk into the marble top, and the rest of it was elaborately encased to hide the supply and drain pipes. In many cases, even after the arrival of running water, it continued to reside in the bedroom, though the bathroom and the dressing room were also likely spots. It acquired a new name: the lavatory.

Technically, in America, *lavatory* refers to the washbasin or sink, although it is also sometimes used to refer to the bathroom. (In Britain, *lavatory* is used to refer to the toilet; although in nineteenth-century Britain it meant the washbasin and its cabinet, what we would now call a vanity.) A wide range of designs for lavatories was available, from fairly simple ones that sat on wall brackets, to large double-bowl lavatories with more decoration than a dining room sideboard. The basins (generally china) were usually plain white, but could be ordered with colored underglaze decorations such as flowers, classical motifs, Oriental or Rococo motifs, or whatever happened to be fashionable at the time. Toward the end of the century, under the influence of germ theory and the sanitarians, lavatories became much more simplified, with exposed piping and nickel-plated legs.

RUNNING HOT AND COLD

All of this plumbing would not have become nearly as popular without the invention of easier ways to get hot water to the tubs, sinks, and showers. Indeed, hot and cold running water and indoor toilets are pretty much the hallmark of western civilization. For centuries, if you wanted hot water it had to be heated in the fire or on the stove (introduced in the 1820s). Some of the early water-heating products were scary: a sheet-metal bathtub with an open-flame gas burner underneath, or heaters attached to one end of the tub with no flue to carry off the combustion gases. Eventually hot-water tanks or boilers attached to the stove became the most common way to heat water. This method continued well into the twentieth century. Another method is what we would now call an instantaneous water heater, which uses gas burners to heat the water as it flows through a coiled pipe. Known as "geysers" in Britain, the first of these was invented in 1868 by Benjamin Maughan. It had a tendency to blow up, lacking important safety features such as a pilot light or a thermostat, but these flaws were eventually corrected. This kind of water heater

Water heater

produce an endless supply of hot water, it's an all-or-nothing proposition—a trickle of hot water is not possible. The invention of the temperature and pressure-release valve in the late 1930s eliminated the danger of water heater explosions and made them safer for home use.

RING AROUND THE CHOLERA

No history of nineteenth-century plumbing would be complete without a discussion of sewage. Although it had been known for several centuries that it was not a good idea to foul the drinking water with human or animal waste, it wasn't until the nineteenth century that anything serious was done about it, and it was still an uphill battle. (In fact, the battle continues in many parts of the world today.) The fact that the subject could not be discussed in polite society made it all the more difficult.

Early in the nineteenth century, five-hundred thousand people in Britain were dying every year from preventable ailments caused by their living conditions. Although there were drains and sewers of sorts in larger towns and cities, bad or ignorant workmanship and poor maintenance often meant these did more harm than good. They still drained into the rivers and streams that were also the source of drinking water, or leaking cesspits polluted the groundwater, making well water unsafe also. Most sewers were made of rough brick and were large enough to stand up in. (Think of the sewers of Paris in the movie version of *Les Miserables*.) There was insufficient water to flush them, so the sewage didn't move. Cesspits were still common, and old ones were often just covered over instead of removed. Things might have gone on being this bad except for the coming of cholera. Long believed to be an Asiatic disease that would not dare infect a decent Englishman, it struck first in 1832 and at intervals until 1866. Although the bacterium that

continues to be more common in Europe than in the United States. Many of the early-twentieth-century instantaneous water heaters are still in use. Some of them are quite beautiful, with Art Nouveau casting and nickel trim. But we opted for the rather wasteful gas- or electric-heated storage tank, which has been likened to leaving your car running all the time in case you might want to go somewhere. Instantaneous heaters also have a major drawback: although they causes cholera was not identified until later in the century, it was already known that contaminated water was the most common means of dissemination. This is also true of typhoid, another disease spread by polluted water. In 1842, Edwin Chadwick, one of the most prominent reformers of the day, wrote a report detailing the atrocious sanitary conditions all over Britain. He believed that cholera was caused by the filth in the streets and the privies, and that a good drainage system with nonabsorbent stoneware pipes would put an end to cholera. He was correct, but he (and others) had to lobby Parliament and various other authorities for years before anything was actually done. In 1846, Sir Henry Doulton opened a factory to make the new glazed-stoneware pipes that would make functional drains possible. But it was not until 1858 that the Metropolitan Board of Works was founded and began the enormous task of laying one thousand miles of new sewers beneath London. The new system opened in 1865, and within five years the death rate in London began to fall significantly. Possibly this was due not only to the sewers, but to the fact that the drinking water was now being brought from the presumably cleaner upstream parts of the Thames.

In the United States, sanitation took a little longer to get off the ground (or into it, as the case may be). Although sanitary reformers in the 1840s and 1850s had urged Americans to upgrade their sanitation practices, their agenda was moral reform, targeting poverty and behavioral degeneracy as threats to public health. After the Civil War, the concept of sanitary science changed. Rather than stressing behavior modification, sanitarians began to insist that sanitation was based on scientific principles and therefore affected everyone. The existing sewers and drains, like Britain's, were large enough to stand in and were made of rough brick. Most had originally been built to carry off surface water rather than sewage. (We eventually wised up to this and now have two different

systems: storm drains, though sometimes referred to as sewers, are larger drains that carry surface run-off; sewers are smaller pipes that carry sewage to treatment plants.) By the 1870s, the dreaded "sewer gas" had been personified as the enemy in the sanitary crusade. It was blamed for every imaginable ill, and near-hysterical warnings about "miasmas" and "foul vapors" emanating from bad drains, fixtures, and sewers filled the media of the time. This was in spite of the fact that both cholera and typhoid were known to be caused by contaminated water. (Even today, typhoid kills 600,000 people every year, mostly in developing countries, because of inadequate sanitation.) The rhetoric became quite heated, with sanitarians, architects, builders, homeowners, and plumbers all blaming each other for buildings that were now viewed as "death traps."

In the 1870s, many municipalities began to install sewers. By the 1880s, it was finally agreed upon that each fixture must have its own trap, each drain must be vented through the roof, and the drains must run downhill at a certain slant, which is the system we still use. Sanitarians also recommended that fixtures be left open with exposed and accessible pipes rather than enclosed in cabinetwork. George Waring wrote in 1881 that water closets should be made of "white earthenware . . . standing as a white vase in a floor of white tiles . . . open to inspection and ventilation," while an 1885 *Good Housekeeping* article assured readers that "white encaustic tiles" would ensure "bright appearance, superior cleanliness, and purity." The sanitarians lobbied for municipal oversight of plumbing, which eventually led to the adoption of detailed plumbing codes in both cities and small towns.

The general acceptance of Louis Pasteur's "germ theory" of disease in the 1880s (it had been known for some time, but there was much argument about and resistance to it) also set the stage for the late-nineteenth and early-twentieth-century obsession with

By 1899, the sanitary idea was firmly entrenched, as shown in this mostly white bathroom at the Dunsmuir House in Oakland, California. The marble slab is now open underneath the sink, the walls are lined with white subway tiles (albeit with a lovely shell design border), and another marble slab on the floor under the sink contains a separate drain for any water that might spill.

hygiene. Though the sanitarians' urgings about open fixtures were not immediately heeded, by the turn of the twentieth century they had become the norm.

ANAEROBICS CLASS

Although sewers were rapidly becoming the norm, in rural and many suburban areas, septic tanks and cesspools were the most common ways of dealing with sewage. Cesspools continued to be used well into the twentieth century, up to the 1950s, but have been regulated out of existence. A cesspool is basically a large brick, stone, or concrete vault where solids can settle. Eventually it fills up and has to be

pumped out. Many cesspools were converted to septic tanks as regulations changed. A septic tank is a whole system consisting of a watertight, underground tank or tanks designed to capture solid wastes, and a disposal field laid out to disperse the liquid wastes. In the septic tank, anaerobic bacteria (bacteria that live in the absence of air) break down the solid wastes, which settle to the bottom. The lighter liquid wastes rise to the top, where they exit through a pipe into a dispersal field consisting of perforated or open-jointed pipes buried in shallow, gravel-filled trenches. Any remaining bacteria and organic matter is (theoretically) absorbed and broken down by the soil before the liquid percolates down to groundwater supplies. A septic tank also has to be pumped out periodically or the solid wastes will build up until they spill into the disposal field, creating a serious health hazard. Septic tanks continue to be used in areas where there are no sewers.

By the end of the nineteenth century, many American cities and towns had not only integrated water supply and sewer systems but also gas piping and electric power. All the elements for a modern bathroom were in place, and with the exception of a few technical improvements and the introduction of water-saving toilets, most of the changes to the bathroom in the twentieth century were cosmetic.

CLEAN ON ME

By 1900, the sanitary idea was firmly entrenched, as it were, though not universally. But indoor plumbing with hot and cold running water was rapidly becoming the norm in urban and suburban areas, although, as with most things, it came first to the wealthy and the middle class, and much later to the poor. Rural areas took a while to catch up, but by mid-century, the majority of Americans enjoyed the benefits of indoor plumbing and sanitation. By 1907,

Although another bathroom at the 1904 Riordan House features an embossed toilet, this high-tank toilet is smooth and easy to clean, just like the sanitarians recommended. It is flanked by a rolled-rim wall-hung sink, as well as some shallow cabinets and a freestanding towel rack. An electrical outlet is mounted high on the wall—not very handy for actually plugging things in.

almost every city in America had sewers. In 1901, New York passed the Model Tenement House Reform law, requiring water to be provided to every floor of new buildings and to each apartment. This was emulated by other cities, and since law already required plumbing, many builders had incentive to install bathtubs and toilets as well.

All toilet designs from the nineteenth century, except for the pan closet, continued to be sold, but the siphon-jet and wash-down models were more popular (eventually the siphon-jet won out entirely). Although some nineteenth-century toilets had been made of enameled cast iron, by the twentieth century, vitreous china had become the material of choice for the bowls and often the tanks as well, though wooden tanks were still offered. Here is a description of the vitreous china firing process from a 1911 plumbing catalog:

Proportions of foreign and domestic clays, feldspar, and flint are used in a mixture of which the fixture is molded. When seasoned, the form is placed in the kiln where the temperature is raised to over 2,000 degrees. When the ware has been sufficiently fired, the kiln is allowed to cool slowly and the ware or "biscuit" is removed. The "biscuit" is then scoured to remove roughness and

dipped in a solution composed of flint, spar, oxide of lead, and other components that comprise the glaze. The glazed "biscuit" is again returned to the kiln and fired to a fusing point, the body and glaze becoming vitrified into one material, not an earthenware body with a glazed finish.

But these were no longer the gloriously decorated toilets of the nineteenth century, with their relief patterns, lions, and hand painting. Hygiene had won the day, so early-twentieth-century toilets were smooth, white, and easy to clean. Both high- and low-tank models were available, though eventually, the low tank became more popular.

In 1911, the Kohler Company introduced the one-piece double-wall tub, which we still use. Before this, built-in baths were cast in two pieces, the tub itself and the apron. These were either fitted together by the plumber during installation, or welded together at the factory before enameling. The one-piece design eliminated crevices, which was more sanitary. Other manufacturers followed suit. Solid porcelain tubs continued to be made as well. Peripheral items such as footbaths, sitz baths, and shower "receptors" came in both porcelain and enameled cast iron. Eventually the five-foot-long double-wall tub in a niche became the standard installation, as it continues to be today.

A shower over a tub in the 1901 Stimson-Green Mansion in Seattle, Washington, is guaranteed to keep one's hair dry and the rest of the room wet.

Showers were eventually simplified from the elaborate cages of the nineteenth century, and the plumbing for them began to be concealed inside the wall, though visible pipes didn't die out entirely. As bathrooms shrank, the space-saving combination tub/shower became more common. Generally the shower had separate controls from the tub faucet, and the more expensive models had anti-scald valves similar to those used today. Both tubs and showers featured mixing valves, even while sinks continued to have separate taps. The shower was still viewed not so much as a means of cleanliness but more as health-related. Ad copy of the time used words like "invigorating," "bracing," and "energizing." And showers were thought more appropriate for men, as women were still considered too "delicate" to be invigorated.

In 1926, the Universal Sanitary Manufacturing Company pioneered colored porcelain. The Kohler Company, which announced a line of six colors in 1927, followed them, and the Crane Company introduced a line of eighteen colors in 1928, six of which were marbleized. Matching color in vitreous and enameled cast-iron fixtures was a huge technological achievement since they require different raw materials and processes. These first experiments with color were all in pastel tones. By the 1930s, everyone had jumped onto the bandwagon, and more intense colors like red and black were added to the pastels. White, however, was and continues to be the most popular color for bathroom fixtures.

In the 1930s, there was an emphasis on streamlining and Art Deco–influenced designs, although it was still possible to buy a claw-foot bathtub. In part, the new designs and colors were desperate attempts to increase sales during the Great Depression. American Standard introduced the Neo-Angle Tub in 1935, claiming "the sensational, entirely new Neo-Angle, which in a few months revolutionized bathroom planning. If distinction and convenience are both essential, you must decide on the Neo-Angle. No other bath is such an all-purpose, all-age, all-condition bath."

Due to the Great Depression, the distribution of the majority of these fixtures was delayed until after World War II, so many of them were not actually installed until the 1940s and '50s. The 1920s and '30s also saw the introduction of new wall-cladding materials such as structural glass. Opaque structural glass slabs were first developed around 1900 as a more sanitary alternative to marble for wainscoting and countertops. Originally offered only in white and black, by the late 1930s it was available in more than thirty colors, including pastels, jewel tones, and agate and marble-like striations. It could be bent, carved, inlaid, and sandblasted, and ranged from semitransparent to opaque. It fit in well with the new aesthetics of the Art Deco and Modern movements. Although structural glass was produced by at least eight different companies, the market was dominated by two brand names, Carrara and Vitrolite. While structural glass is far more common on storefronts, it was installed in some bathrooms, though it never attained the popularity of tile.

Remodeling of this 1914 bathroom in the 1930s replaced its original white sanitary look with an Art Deco look, featuring the American Standard "Towerlyn" pedestal sink, "Teriston" toilet, and "Pembroke" tub in Ming Green. Unusual window muntin patterns are a feature of this Prairie-style bungalow. New Pratt and Larson floor tile replaced ugly sheet flooring added by a previous owner, and the wall tile is also new.

Sinks didn't change much until the late 1930s. Up to that time, under-mount basins and wall-hung and pedestal sinks were the norm, although there were a few sinks set into cabinets, like modern vanities. There is very little difference in design between a sink from 1910 and a sink from the early 1930s. A newer sink is more likely to have a mixing-style faucet, which had been available for some time but didn't seem to be used on sinks at that time. Sinks tended to have separate taps, perhaps because people were still using them like the old-fashioned washbasins, filling them up with water for washing rather than using running water. Manufacturers also made an attempt to sell small extra sinks, called dental sinks, to be used

A remodel in the 1930s left the 1901 Colonial Revival Warfield House in Elkins, West Virginia, with two stunning Art Deco bathrooms paneled in Marlite (a less-expensive pressed wood-and-plastic alternative to structural glass) and trimmed with horizontal strips of chrome for the streamlined look popular during the Art Deco period. (Photo © Stephen J. Shaluta, Jr.)

only for toothbrushing purposes, but these didn't really catch on.

Other items that didn't really catch on in America included bidets, special drinking fountain spouts for bathroom sinks, floor toilets (basically a porcelain-lined hole in the floor with plumbing that flushes with a foot pedal—these are still common in many parts of the world), and "baby toilets" (only ten inches high). Other items, such as footbaths, sitz baths, and needle showers, eventually stopped being sold, partly because bathrooms became smaller and partly because they were no longer popular.

One thing that did catch on was the "powder room," traditionally a half-bath (sink and toilet) for the use of guests. Originally recommended to be off the dining room, it was much more likely to be installed under the stairs, off the entry, or off the hall-way. Another location was the utility porch, where it was to be used by servants, workmen, or those wash-ing up when coming in from the garden.

As the century progressed, bathrooms became more standardized. Changes to fixtures were primarily cosmetic. A few technological changes have taken place, such as the invention of the single-handle faucet (patented by Al Moen in 1942), the whirlpool tub (introduced by Jacuzzi in 1968), plastic piping, and, more recently, the water-saving toilet. Elaborate showers, reminiscent of nineteenth-century models, are now known as "vertical whirlpools" and even include waterfall-type showerheads, allowing us to experience what our early ancestors knew, only with hot water. But a modern bathroom is not that differ-ent from its early-twentieth-century predecessor, which is perhaps why quite a few historic bathrooms have survived untouched.

Various brands of vintage sheet toilet paper, including Nabob, Sheplark, Victorian, Crescent, and Blue Tint, are displayed beneath an advertisement for American Standard bathtubs. (Courtesy of Vintage Plumbing.)

SOAP'S UP

"Clean hands and hearts may hope

To find the way to happiness

By using lots of soap."

—From a 1920s pamphlet distributed at schools by the Cleanliness Institute (later used by Proctor and Gamble to advertise Ivory Soap)

The history of toilet paper, soap, toothbrushes, razors, and other bathroom items is worth delving into briefly. Toilet tissue was unknown before the nineteenth century. Ancient peoples used shells, leaves, or bunches of herbs. Wealthy Romans used sponges, which were kept in a container of salt water. In medieval times, small pieces of cloth cut from worn-out garments were sometimes employed. In many cultures, the hand is utilized (not as bad as it sounds—usually water is involved as well). Toilet paper first made its appearance in 1857, when Joseph

An Art Nouveau–influenced holder dispenses toilet paper at the 1908 Gamble House.

C. Gayetty introduced "Gayetty's Medicated Paper— a perfectly pure article for the toilet and for the prevention of piles." It was made from hemp. Throughout the nineteenth century, toilet paper was supplied in individual sheets, which were kept in a box that sat on the back of the water closet. After perforated toilet paper on a roll was introduced around 1880, new types of holders were designed to accommodate it.

Tissue in sheets continued to be produced, but mostly fell into disfavor in the twentieth century. Of course, people who still had outhouses customarily used other things that were lying around, such as corncobs (soaked in water to soften them) and pages from the Sears Roebuck or Montgomery Ward catalog.

Before the invention of soap, various other things were used for cleansing, including oil and sand, and various "soapweeds." Eventually someone figured out that combining fat or oil with potash (potassium hydroxide or lye) would produce a substance that worked very well for getting things clean, i.e., soap. Soap is still made from these same ingredients. Initially soap was homemade, but it began to be produced commercially in the fourteenth century. Rose petals, lavender, herbs, and other perfumes were added. In 1789, Andrew Pears began making transparent soap by dissolving ordinary soap in alcohol, distilling it to produce a transparent jelly that was then dried in molds. (Pears's Soap is still made.) Until the nineteenth century, soap was used far more often for washing clothes than for washing humans. The invention of detergents in the early twentieth century led to the development of shampoo as well as laundry detergent. The first hair dryers were marketed in 1920; made of metal with a wooden handle, they were heavy and had a tendency to overheat, but very much resembled modern blow dryers. Hair dryers were one of the first small appliances to benefit from the use of plastics (such as Bakelite).

Razors go back to Roman times (and probably farther), when they were made of bronze. In the thirteenth century, razors from Brittany are mentioned as being essential to a lady's toilet. The "cut-throat," or straight razor, dates to the fifteenth century and has changed little since then. It was more common to be shaved at a barbershop right up to the turn of the twentieth century. In 1901, King Gillette invented the safety razor. The improvement of shaving was not really his motivation; rather, he wanted something thousands of people would use, that had to be replaced as often as possible, but was so cheap in small quantities that no one would notice the cost over a long period of time. In other words, he invented "planned obsolescence." The safety razor became so common that special slots were placed in the backs of recessed medicine cabinets for the disposal of used blades.

The earliest toothbrushes were simply small sticks that were mashed at one end to increase the cleaning surface. The bristle brush was probably invented by the Chinese (like everything else), and toothpaste can also be traced to China and India as far back as 500 B.C. The bristle brush was introduced to Europe in the seventeenth century and was widely used, especially in France, which had the most advanced dentistry at the time. Cleaning between the teeth with a piece of silk thread was advocated as early as 1815, but dental floss (made of unwaxed silk) did not become commercially available until 1882. Floss was not used by most people until after World War II, when nylon floss became available.

Sheffield's Creme Dentifrice

Compounds for cleaning teeth (and freshening breath) go back thousands of years. Early Egyptian, Chinese, Greek, and Roman writings describe various mixtures for both pastes and powders. Some of the more palatable ingredients included powdered fruit, burnt shells, talc, honey, and dried flowers. Somewhat less appetizing ingredients were also used,

which will not be detailed here. American settlers in the late seventeenth century used a mixture of brimstone, butter, and gunpowder. Modern toothpastes began to appear in the nineteenth century. Dr. Sheffield's Creme Dentifrice, introduced in 1850, became very popular and in 1892 was offered in a collapsible tube, which remains the standard packaging for toothpaste.

LESS IS MORRIS

I would like to think that the Arts and Crafts movement had some influence on bathroom design, and that the simplification called for by its proponents influenced even this humble room. However, there is no evidence to suggest this was the case. At the time of the Arts and Crafts movement in England in the late nineteenth century, Victorian sensibilities didn't allow discussion of such matters in polite society. William Morris was not calling for better toilet design. There may have been some influence on bathroom decor, since Victorian-era bathrooms were often elaborately decorated in the prevailing styles. Stained-glass windows, elaborate tile work, wallpaper, and oriental carpets were all features of Victorian bathrooms. But the simplification of bathrooms had to do with sanitation, not philosophy. Certainly the simpler, "sanitary" bathroom fit right in with the bungalows and other Arts and Crafts–era houses built in America between 1900 and 1930, but the same sort of bathroom was common to all early-twentieth-century houses, and it would be impossible to deduce the architectural style of the house from looking at the bathroom. Most bathrooms fitting the definition of "Arts and Crafts" (with the sort of art tile usually found on fireplaces) were not installed till the very late 1920s or the 1930s, after the movement itself had died out. There were no matte-green toilets, no washbasins hand painted with stylized flowers, and no appliquéd shower curtains. (More's the pity—wouldn't a Rookwood toilet be fabulous?) Yet these bathrooms, with simple white tile and fixtures, or exuberantly colored tile and fixtures, are still remarkably usable by modern standards. Our expectations have changed a little: we are more likely to view the bathroom as a retreat, not just a place to bathe and brush our teeth; we prefer to have more than one bathroom; we like to have two sinks if we're sharing; and certainly bathrooms in new houses have all kinds of bells and whistles like fireplaces and whirlpool tubs. But our fixation with cleanliness differs little from the early-twentieth-century obsession with sanitation. Because plumbing technology has changed so little, a bungalow bathroom is still perfectly functional for the twenty-first century.

Aesthetic Movement decorating influences are shown in an 1889 bathroom addition to an 1878 Italianate Victorian. While the marble-topped corner lavatory is original to the room, the rest had to be re-created. A salvaged medicine cabinet and high-tank toilet, new hexagonal-tile floor, bead-board wainscoting salvaged from old garage doors, and a stained-glass window from a church are combined with embossed Anaglypta wallpaper and a stenciled border at the ceiling for the full Victorian treatment.

Nuts and Bolts

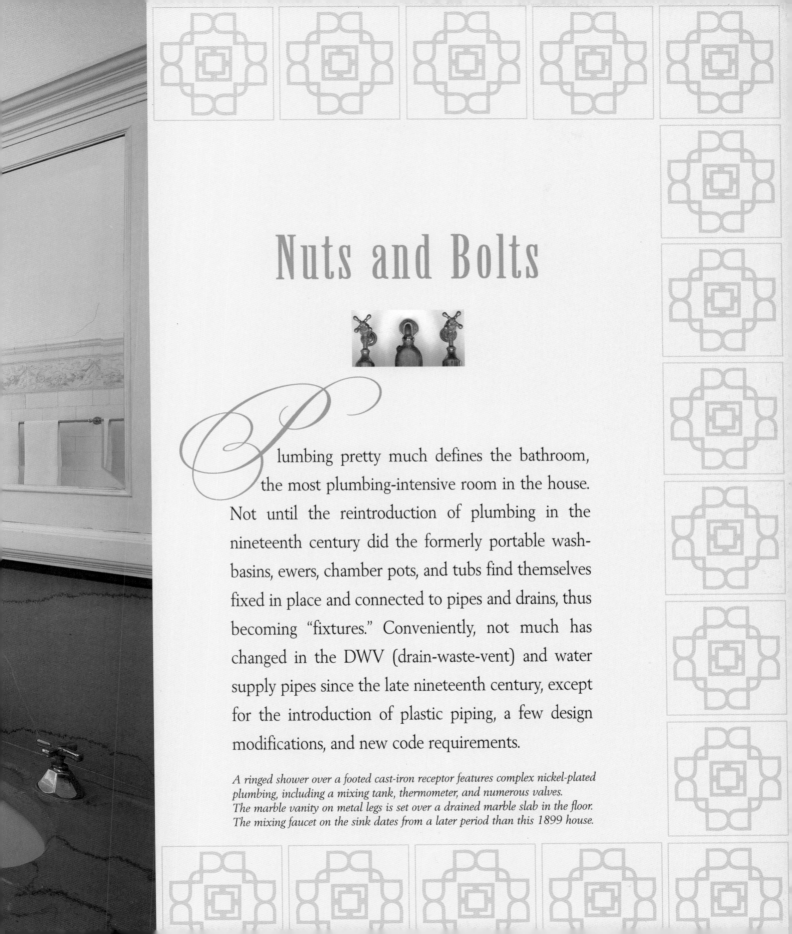

Plumbing pretty much defines the bathroom, the most plumbing-intensive room in the house. Not until the reintroduction of plumbing in the nineteenth century did the formerly portable washbasins, ewers, chamber pots, and tubs find themselves fixed in place and connected to pipes and drains, thus becoming "fixtures." Conveniently, not much has changed in the DWV (drain-waste-vent) and water supply pipes since the late nineteenth century, except for the introduction of plastic piping, a few design modifications, and new code requirements.

A ringed shower over a footed cast-iron receptor features complex nickel-plated plumbing, including a mixing tank, thermometer, and numerous valves. The marble vanity on metal legs is set over a drained marble slab in the floor. The mixing faucet on the sink dates from a later period than this 1899 house.

Supply Side Economics

Water enters the house either from a public water main or a source on the property. City water is usually delivered through a meter and a main shutoff valve. The meter may be in the basement or crawl space, or outdoors near the property line. If it is outdoors, a buried pipe usually runs from there to the house. Sometimes there is a main shutoff valve near where the line enters the house, or near the meter; sometimes the shutoff valve is at the meter itself. After entering the house, the main supply line splits in two: one remaining cold and going to the cold-water outlets, the other going off to the water heater and then to the various hot-water outlets.

The DWV pipes use gravity to channel wastewater and solid wastes to the main house drain, which connects to the sewer line or septic tank (thus the plumbers' adage "S**t flows downhill"). The vent pipes disperse the dreaded sewer gas into the atmosphere and maintain air pressure in drainpipes and fixture traps (traps are curved sections in the drainpipes that remain water-filled to prevent gases from coming up through the drains). Every house has a main soil stack (usually in the vicinity of a toilet, since toilets require the biggest drainpipes), which serves as the primary drainpipe below the level of the fixtures and as a vent above the fixtures. Drainpipes from other fixtures and branch drains from other bathrooms connect to the main stack. Another bathroom on a branch drain away from the main stack will have a secondary vent stack of its own. Often the main soil stack is found inside a deeper-than-normal wall (2 x 4s wouldn't accommodate it) or a specially-built chase (a diagonal corner in a bathroom), or recessed into an adjoining closet; however, in a house that's seen a lot of remodeling, particularly if bathrooms were added, the soil stack may be running up an outside wall.

Pipe Dream

Pipes of extruded lead, first used around 1850, had drawbacks, including heaviness and a tendency toward leaks caused by sagging. (At the time, there was no knowledge of the dangers of lead poisoning.) Later in the nineteenth century, cast iron, galvanized iron, copper, and brass replaced lead except in certain applications. All these materials (except lead) are still in use. It is still possible to remove an old toilet and find a lead "closet bend" leading to the drainpipe. Recently, plastic piping, either PVC (polyvinyl chloride—the white stuff) or ABS (the black stuff) has been added to the list, as well as flexible plastic tubing (PEX), which has yet to find wide acceptance in the U.S. but is used extensively in Europe.

Copper supply pipes are still the highest-quality pipes one can have, and also the most expensive. The soldered joints (solder is metal that melts at a fairly low temperature and flows into the spaces between the pipe and the fitting, making it watertight) require more skill to put together, and the copper itself is expensive. But copper pipes don't corrode like galvanized metal, and therefore last a very long time. It is usually a good idea (and easy) to replace galvanized pipes if the wall is open for some other reason. If pipes are being replaced, it is worthwhile to use copper; however, where copper joins with existing galvanized pipes, be sure to use a *dielectric fitting*, which separates the two different kinds of metal to prevent galvanic corrosion (a wild orgy of molecular exchange between dissimilar metals).

In most early-twentieth-century houses, supply pipes are likely to be galvanized steel. Rather than soldered, galvanized pipes are threaded and use threaded fittings. Watertightness is enhanced through the use of "pipe dope" on the threads or, these days, Teflon tape. Galvanized pipe has gotten a bad name because after seventy or eighty years, interior corrosion tends to restrict water flow, reducing water pressure; eventually, corrosion makes its way through the pipe wall, causing leaks. (The iron in galvanized pipes is also responsible for the pinkish residue that builds up on the walls of bathrooms that are not well ventilated; after the water evaporates, small amounts of iron remain.) Hot-water pipes tend to corrode more, and horizontal runs of pipe collect more crud than vertical runs. This does not necessarily mean that all the pipes need replacement. Sometimes replacing only the hot-water pipes will work wonders to restore water pressure.

Plastic pipe is a more recent development. Either PVC (white) or ABS (black) is commonly used (there seem to be regional differences). Plastic pipe joints and fittings are glued, making it easier to work with than copper. It is not as rigid as metal pipe, and tends to sag in horizontal runs if not supported. In some localities, plastic pipe is not allowed by code, while in others, it is required.

DRAIN OF TERROR

The water coming in through the supply pipes also needs an escape route once it has served its purpose, and the DWV system allows the used water and other waste to make its way to the sewer or septic tank while maintaining air pressure in the system, preventing the contamination of clean water with used water, and guarding against the dreaded "sewer gas" by venting it through the roof. The subject of much experimentation in the nineteenth century, the DWV system hasn't changed much since then. In the early twentieth century, while visible drainpipes were usually nickel- or chrome-plated brass or copper, once inside the wall, cast-iron drainpipes were the rule. Joints came together with "hub" or "bell and spigot" fittings, joined with molten lead and oakum (hemp or jute impregnated with asphalt). Today,

A nickel-plated "bottle" trap with clean-out plug and two cross-handled supply valves with air chambers form part of the plumbing for an antique lavatory. (Courtesy of Vintage Plumbing.)

A chain-operated louvered vent allows steam to escape from this bath at the 1911 Lanterman House.

A painted electric wall fixture with an etched-glass shade is installed at the Lanterman House. Builders often installed both gas and electric fixtures.

neoprene gaskets held by adjustable stainless-steel clamps have replaced this method.

CURRENT EVENTS

Most houses in urban areas had electricity by the early part of the twentieth century, so bathrooms were wired for electric lights and plugs along with the rest of the house. In areas that were not electrified until later, there might still be piping for gas lighting. Electric wiring at that time was knob-and-tube. Old wiring is usually fine, provided that the insulation on the wiring is intact and it is not overloaded. A house with 30-amp service and only a few circuits could probably benefit from a service upgrade to 100 amps or more. This will take some of the load off the remaining knob-and-tube wiring.

A bathroom generally only has one circuit, which it may share with adjoining bedrooms or hallways. A small bathroom might have only one light, either mounted in the center of the ceiling or as a sconce over the medicine cabinet or mirror. A larger bathroom might have both a ceiling light and one or more sconces. Generally there was only one electrical outlet, either on the wall or sometimes as part of the sconce; a plug was often fitted into the canopy. Some bathrooms also had electric wall heaters. Light switches were originally push-button, replaced in the late teens or early twenties with brown Bakelite toggle switches similar to those we use today. The fixtures were usually simple. Ceiling-mounted canopies (or occasionally pendants) of nickel or brass with schoolhouse or other simple glass shades were the standard. In a very utilitarian bathroom, such as a half-bath off the utility room, a bare light bulb on a cord was the norm. Sconces were also simple designs in nickel or brass with glass shades, or porcelain with either bare light bulbs or glass shades. These porcelain fixtures were almost exclusively used in bathrooms. Art-glass fixtures and chandeliers are not appropriate for bathrooms, though a chandelier in a bathroom can be amusing. There were no recessed down lights.

In some states, the building code requires the first switched light in the bathroom to be fluorescent as an energy-saving measure. Usually this light has to be hard-wired: putting a compact fluorescent bulb in a regular fixture does not count. This is a difficult problem because most hard-wired fluorescent fixtures do not come in historically appropriate styles, and, although fluorescent lights have improved in color recently, they still look wrong in rooms that were designed to be viewed under incandescent light.

Electricity and water are an inherently dangerous combination, which is why GFCI outlets (ground fault circuit interrupters) are required by the building code for bathrooms. A GFCI will shut off the power in a split second, saving you from electrocution,

Both the porcelain canopy and the glass shade of this Art Deco sconce are trimmed with black pinstriping.

Square sconces were typical Craftsman light fixtures. Bathroom fixtures were usually nickel-plated.

An unusual Muresque-tile light fixture is a good fit for this 1930 bathroom.

although I still would not recommend using a hair dryer while sitting in the tub. It's difficult to cut a hole for a new outlet in an existing tile wainscot, so try to put it above the tile if possible, or in an alternate location such as inside a cabinet.

A lavender porcelain fixture with a stepped Art Deco design matches the lavender tile in a 1932 bathroom.

Obsessive Restoration

A GFCI outlet is still a good idea for safety's sake. The outlet can either be hidden in some way (in cabinetry, in a recessed box, etc.) or a GFCI circuit breaker can be used, protecting the whole circuit and allowing for a regular three-hole outlet.

Try to avoid cutting a new outlet box into existing tile wainscoting, but if you can't avoid it, make sure you know the location of these items before you start:

- Studs
- Electrical wiring
- Water pipes
- Fire blocking

Mask off the surrounding tile with sheet metal or metal flat-bar stock held with double-sided carpet tape or duct tape—this will protect it from damage. Use a diamond blade on a high-speed mini-grinder. There will be dust, sparks, and heat, so have an assistant with a shop vacuum and a spray bottle. Cooling the blades or bits with water will prolong their life, but expect to use more than one. The grinder will not cut all the way into the corners, but a small hammer drill with an eighth-inch carbide bit works well for finishing up, or else a RotoZip or rotary tool. Make a dotted line of perforations in the corners—try not to drill all the way through the tile (put a cork on the

Top left: Fairly ornate for a bathroom, a nickel leaf-patterned sconce flanks a mirror in the 1901 Stimson-Green Mansion in Seattle.
Top right: A hanging sconce at the 1899 Dunsmuir House features a shade etched in a Greek key design.
Bottom: A combination gas and electric wall fixture adorns one bath at the 1899 Dunsmuir House. Combination
fixtures were decidedly unsafe (electric sparks could ignite the gas) but were often used before electricity became dependable.

drill bit for depth control). When the corners are perforated, break them out with a carbide-tipped chisel, available from tile suppliers. An oversized outlet cover will disguise some of the damage if things don't go well. Since there will only be one chance to get it right on the wall, it might be prudent to dummy up some tile set in mortar to practice.

Original light fixtures should obviously be kept if possible. They can be rewired, replated, or repaired as necessary. Many appropriate period fixtures are available at salvage yards and antiques dealers. Reproductions (many cast from original molds) are also a reasonable choice. Electrified versions of gaslights can be purchased as well. Porcelain fixtures were mostly used in the 1920s and 1930s. Push-button light switches and Edison-style vintage lightbulbs are also being reproduced.

Today we seem to require more light than our predecessors did, so it is possible to judiciously add a few more fixtures—particularly sconces around the mirror—without unduly impacting the historic character of the room.

If a hard-wired fluorescent is required by code, probably the most unobtrusive way to do it is to design a square, recessed light with some wood trim around it, as was done by Frank Lloyd Wright or Greene & Greene. For this purpose, the rules could be relaxed enough to allow art glass, which does a wonderful job of disguising the weird pinkish color of "warm white" fluorescents. Of course, the really obvious answer to this problem lies between you and your conscience.

Left & Bottom: An adjustable nickel sconce could either be pointed up for ambient lighting, or down toward the face of the person standing at the sink, by simply slipping the curved rod up or down through the ring.
Top Right: A metal medicine cabinet with fluorescent (or sometimes incandescent) tube lights on either side was typical of the 1930s and beyond.

Compromise Solution

A GFCI can be made less obtrusive by finding one that has TEST/RESET buttons the same color as the outlet, and, for some reason, a horizontal outlet blends in better than a vertical one. As in obsessive restoration, a GFCI breaker can be used instead, and it's best not to cut a new outlet box into tile wainscoting if you can help it. With a GFCI breaker, try to use the regular three-hole outlets rather than the square "décor" outlets, which look too modern.

A chandelier is generally not appropriate to a bathroom (amusing, though) unless the bathroom is awfully grand, such as in a mansion. This three-arm nickel chandelier is at the Dunsmuir House in Oakland, California.

Many fine reproduction fixtures are being made these days, but try to stick with the very simple ones. You can have as many as you like. If your bathroom originally had gaslight, electrified reproductions of gas fixtures are available as well. Art glass, as a rule, was not found in bathrooms, except in windows. If you simply must have a recessed downlight, it should go in the shower or over the tub (there is a special kind that is designed for use in wet areas)—otherwise, stick with sconces and ceiling mounts. Nothing else screams "turn of the twenty-first century" like a recessed can. Try to avoid "light bars"—use a two-arm sconce instead.

A dimmer switch is a fine idea in a bathroom (lessens the shock of turning on the light on those dark mornings or middle-of-the-night forays to the bathroom), and even reproduction push-button switches are available as dimmers.

A decorative pierced tile in a leaf-and-twig design provides passive ventilation in a 1932 bathroom.

AIR TO THE THRONE

Ventilation is important since the bathroom is the source of large amounts of water vapor as well as, how can one put this delicately, odors. Most bathrooms have at least one window, and some will have a passive vent that may run up through the roof, although some open directly into the attic—not a good place for massive amounts of water vapor to congregate. Realistically, a window doesn't work that well for ventilation, because who is going to be willing to open it in the winter? So a fan is the best way to go, though I must admit here that I hate fans. The noise annoys me. The fan needs to be big enough to move the volume of air (measured in cubic feet) in the room. Fans can generate a lot of noise, so try to get the quietest one that you can. Fan noise is rated in sones, and they will be labeled accordingly. A low rating (1 to 2 sones) will be quieter, and a fan with a remote motor will also be quieter.

One bathroom at the 1911 Lanterman House in La Cañada-Flintridge, California, has a gas wall sconce. In 1911, this area was still rural, and electrical service may not have been reliable.

An electric wall heater features visible coiled wires separated by porcelain ridges in a 1930s bath.

Obsessive Restoration

If you're actually willing to open the window in the winter, you can do without a fan, although a window is not as efficient as a fan. If there is an existing passive vent, it is not too hard to retrofit a ventilation fan into it—just make sure it is vented outside and not into the attic. The existing grille can be reused to make it blend in. If a new fan is installed, just replace the ugly plastic grille that accompanies it with a nice metal or wooden register cover instead. Avoid fan/light combinations—the lights are not appropriate, and a cheap plastic housing is usually involved. In a landlocked bathroom with no window, the building code may require the fan to come on with the light—this is annoying and hard to get around. If it is possible to have the fan on a separate switch, it will do much for your sanity.

Compromise Solution

Again, if you're willing to open the window, you can do without a fan. If you're not willing to forgo the light/fan combination, at least get the simplest, most unobtrusive design you can find, and try to mount it somewhere less obvious if possible. Or maybe mount a fan in an outside wall, and hang a hinged piece of art over it that you can open while the fan is on and use to cover it the rest of the time.

Nice detailing graces the register that heats this bath in a 1932 Spanish-style house.

Thermal Underware

Although using it may build character, an unheated bathroom is not pleasant. Many bathrooms were built without heat, relying on heat from elsewhere, such as a floor furnace in the hallway or heat drifting in from other rooms. If you're lucky, your bathroom(s) may have registers, radiators, wall heaters, or even radiant heating in the floor. If not, it might be a good idea to add some heat. The easiest thing to add is a portable electric heater, which is available in various sizes and types such as small, oil-filled radiators, or convection heaters with fans. It's useful to have an extra plug for this. Heat lamps mounted in the ceiling are ugly but especially functional for small bathrooms. Sometimes these can be part of equally ugly built-in ventilation fan/light combos. Small, recessed electric wall heaters that fit between two studs are also possibilities. These require only some new wiring. There are also both electric and hot-water-filled baseboard heaters—a lot of them are quite ugly, but there are some low-profile ones that resemble actual baseboards. Gas wall heaters are also available but will require a flue. Electric heaters are not very cost-efficient for full-time heat but are fine when run for only the few minutes the bathroom is in use.

If there is an existing central hot-air system, it is usually fairly easy to add another run of ducting to the bathroom. The biggest problem may be cutting a hole for it if there is a tile floor or wainscoting. If the hot-air system is gravity (no fan), it may be a problem running a new duct if the bath is far away from the furnace, because not much hot air will get there. It is possible to buy an electric booster fan that fits inside the duct to help with this problem.

It is also easy to add a new radiator to an existing hot-water or steam system. (See Dan Holohan's many fine books, including *The Lost Art of Steam Heating*.) There are both salvaged old radiators and new radia-

A wall-hung radiator is mounted on the subway-tile wainscoting in a 1906 home.

tors that are quite slim in profile, some including towel warmers. Freestanding electric towel warmers can also be purchased.

The ultimate in heating luxury for bathrooms is radiant floor heating, especially for ceramic-tile floors, which tend to be cold. There are both hydronic heating, which uses plastic tubing that circulates heated water under the floor, and electric mats, which use wires, rather like an electric blanket. Either can be embedded in mortar under ceramic tile, and plastic tubing can also be used under wood floors. Hydronic tubing requires a boiler and is probably not cost-effective unless it is being installed throughout the house rather than just in the bathroom. Electric mats come with thermostats and timers, require only wiring, and have the advantage of being relatively inexpensive.

An original electric wall heater with wires spiraling around a porcelain column heats the bathroom of this 1930s home.

would not be out of the question to improve on the original design a little for more comfort. Early electric wall heaters tended to be assemblages of columnar porcelain insulators with electric wire elements twisted around them, hidden behind lovely artistic metal grilles. Many of these are still working and are available at salvage yards, though one should probably have the wiring checked out. They probably don't meet existing code requirements.

A modern electric wall heater will probably look too modern, although it could possibly be fitted out with an old grille. Modern gas wall heaters will have the same problem, although there are old ones to be found.

New ducts for hot air (either forced air or gravity) are easy to add, except for the problem of cutting through a tile floor or wainscoting (see "Electricity" for hints). Salvaged or new period-style register covers are easy to come by.

It is also easy to add new radiators to an existing steam or hot-water system. Try to find salvaged radiators that match the others in the house. Some new period-style radiators are also being manufactured. Modern radiators tend to be a little too sleek-looking.

Hydronic heating can be retrofitted under an existing floor (though this may involve tearing out a ceiling if the bath is on the second floor). Electric mats can only be retrofitted if a new floor is being installed.

Obsessive Restoration

If there is no existing heat in the bathroom, the most obsessive thing to do is leave it that way. In a small house, drifting heat from other rooms or a floor furnace in the hallway outside may be enough. And, of course, there's that character-building aspect to being wet, naked, and freezing. Just add a cold shower for complete self-denial!

A small portable electric heater would have the least impact on a historic bathroom, since it could be easily reversed. But if the rest of the house has heat, it

Compromise Solution

Same rules mostly apply as above. Anything modern should be as plain and unobtrusive as possible. Try to avoid the really ugly baseboard heaters. But if you want, you can wrap hydronic tubing around the bathtub to keep the water from getting cold.

Eye Appeal

Standing beneath the canopy you are engulfed by terrifying aquabatics. 'Douche' is a great dagger-like stream, which feels like an apple corer boring through your head, whereas 'Spray' surrounds you with some 200 sharp needles of water. 'Shower' is straightforward, but 'Jet' is like a ramrod up your privates, and 'Sitz' is a gentle fountain for the same delicate area! 'Plunge' fills the bath, gushing out water from a slit, at knee level—and then there is 'Wave,' which sends a flattened jet of water from one side of the room to the other!"

⸺A description by Lucinda Lambton of Shanks Patent "Eureka" Bath, as installed in Kinloch Castle, 1901.

A footed bathtub with a telephone shower, round pedestal sink, and embossed wash-down toilet combine with simple woodwork in the DeForest House, designed by architects Charles and Henry Greene in 1906.

FIXTURE PERFECT

Most older bathrooms include a tub, a sink, and a toilet. Often, and especially in earlier baths, the toilet is in a separate room by itself. Sinks were also installed in bedrooms or closets. In fact, in the nineteenth century, bathrooms were often fit into existing areas of the house, such as closets or under stairways, in an addition onto the back or on a utility porch. If the only bathroom is on the utility porch, it's often a sign that the house didn't originally have indoor plumbing. Some baths may include other fixtures, such as stall showers, bidets, footbaths, or sitz baths. Separate stall showers were a fairly common feature, especially in the 1920s and 1930s, even in modest homes. Foot or sitz baths and bidets were far less common, usually found in grander homes with larger bathrooms. Bidets have never really caught on in the United States, and usually people first encounter them on a trip to Europe. Many manufacturers' catalogs and advertisements show bathrooms with a full complement of fixtures, but it's important to keep in mind that these were sales tools, and do not necessarily reflect the installed reality.

Until the late nineteenth century, most "sanitary ware" was imported from English potteries. After much experimentation, American potteries caught up and began producing their own. (It's much more difficult to make a toilet than a vase.) In fact, initially, toilets were made by hand rather than being molded. It's no wonder Thomas Maddock had only a 10-percent success rate on his first attempts. Methods for firing porcelain enamel onto cast iron were also improved.

Because plumbing fixtures change slowly, it is not always possible to date a bathroom by the fixtures. There are some very general tendencies, but an all-white bathroom could come from just about any period. A Victorian bathroom could have anything from a claw-foot tub to a wood-paneled tub, a wall-hung rolled rim sink or an elaborate vanity, a decorated toilet or a plain one, bead-board wainscoting or tile wainscoting, a wood floor or a tile floor. From the turn of the twentieth century till about 1910, the all-white sanitary bathroom was dominant, yet the fixtures might be the same as the Victorian bath. In the teens, a little color started to sneak in, mostly in the form of tile borders in a white ground. By the early 1920s, wildly colored tile was starting to be used (although there were still plenty of white bathrooms), but the fixtures remained white. In the late 1920s, colored fixtures were perfected, and then things became completely zany with colored fixtures, colored tile, art tile, structural glass, streamlining, new Art Deco–influenced fixture designs, and so forth. This continued into the 1940s and 1950s.

A Cal-Art tile border of water lilies combines with pink field tile, coved black baseboard tile, and a mottled green floor with a green-and-black diamond border in this 1929 bathroom. An oval pedestal sink on a simple round base, a tile-in bathtub, and a toilet (not shown) complete this small 5-by-8-foot bath.

A marble lavatory with marble backsplash rests on fancy nickel-plated legs in a sanitary bathroom at the Stimson-Green Mansion in Seattle, completed in 1901. A flask, or bottle, trap—rather than the usual P-trap— is used for the drain. An ornate radiator sits on the porcelain hexagonal tile floor.

Basin Street

Descended from the Victorian-era washbasin and pitcher, the first sinks were simply traditional washbasins set into a washstand-like piece of furniture and attached to a drain. These often had elaborate carving or decoration in both the washstand and the sink itself (although, as is still true today, most sinks were white). The same techniques used to embellish tableware and ornamental porcelain were applied to sanitary ware. Clay bodies were impressed with relief decoration, fired with transfer-printed patterns, and/or highlighted with gold. The decorations sometimes had an aquatic theme, although the vocabulary of classical ornament was also exploited, probably to evoke the legendary baths of the Romans. Elaborate tiled back-splashes were also common. Later sinks evolved into bowls set into a stone (usually marble) slab, or set into a tiled countertop. These sat on either brackets or legs, although vanity-like cabinets were also found. Wall-hung sinks with rolled rims, which hung on a heavy cast-iron wall bracket or sat on decorative brackets of metal or porcelain, first made an appearance around the turn of the twentieth century. Pedestal sinks of either china or porcelain over cast iron appeared about the same time. Both wall-hung and pedestal sinks often had integral backsplashes. Sinks set into cabinets (like modern vanities) were less common than wall-hung or pedestal sinks but were still fre-quently found, especially in the 1920s and '30s. After the turn of the century, sinks were simplified to gen-erally white, with plumbing usually exposed, in the name of sanitation. Colored sinks began to appear in the late 1920s, after colored porcelain was perfected in 1926 by the Universal Sanitary Manufacturing Company of New Castle, Pennsylvania. The Kohler Company followed in 1927, announcing six new col-ors: Autumn Brown, Lavender, Spring Green, Old Ivory, West Point Gray, and Horizon Blue. Crane

A lavender pedestal sink in a square design is enhanced by turquoise-and-lavender-tile wainscoting featuring a decorative stripe of mosaic tiles in assorted pastels. A mosaic tile floor in a woven pattern, a separate tiled stall shower (to right of sink), a matching lavender tub and toilet (not shown), and chrome-plated wall sconces make for a stylish bathroom in this Spanish-style house.

Plumbing introduced a line of eighteen colors in 1928. Most of the 1920s colors were pastels, while more-vibrant colors appeared in the 1930s. Many of the colors introduced in the 1930s didn't actually appear in bathrooms till the late 1940s and early '50s, delayed because of the depression and World War II.

Most sinks that were set into a counter or stone slab were under-mounted using plaster of Paris and metal clips, although sinks that sat on top of the counter like modern self-rimming sinks were often seen as well. The most prevalent shape was oval, though round, square, or rectangular shapes were also popular. Generally these basins were china rather than enameled cast iron. Cast iron appeared more often in rolled-rim sinks that hung on the wall, though enam-eled pedestal sinks of cast iron were also common. Wall-hung or pedestal sinks could also be made of china.

Neoclassic fluting dresses up the columnar base of an oval pedestal sink at the 1901 Stimson-Green Mansion. A white hexagonal-tile floor and white subway-tiled walls make this the epitome of a "sanitary" bath.

Whatever size the bathroom space, there was a sink made to fit it. Both pedestal and wall-hung sinks came in sizes ranging from tiny powder-room models to huge double-bowl models for grand bathrooms, to space-saving corner models. With either under-mount or self-rimming sinks, the slab or counter could be made as large or as small as was necessary, and could sit on either legs or a cabinet. Some catalog and magazine illustrations showed installations with two sinks, but this was the exception rather than the rule.

Pedestal sinks evolved from nineteenth-century lavatories, which often had decorative shields to hide the drainpipe. By the twentieth century, a few basic styles had evolved, and these changed very little until the 1930s, when the influence of Art Deco caused them to become more stylized. Rectangular or oval were the favored shapes for the tops, and the pedestals tended to be either columnar (often with classical detailing) or squarish. Another model had a wall-hung basin held up by a skinny, baluster-like

pedestal (rather like a ballet dancer *en pointe*). With the exception of the wall-hung models, most pedestal sinks were freestanding. Modern reproductions generally attach to the wall for more stability.

Probably because they evolved from washstands, which are customarily table height (about thirty inches), sinks were, and still are, mounted at that height. The bathroom was not scientifically studied in regard to ergonomics as the kitchen was, at least not until the 1970s, and even those studies had very little influence.

A skinny pedestal requires the bowl to be held up by brackets, as in this 5-by-7-foot turquoise bathroom in a 1932 Art Deco apartment building. Extra black tile has been added to make the shower more waterproof, and the 1950s vintage medicine cabinet does not look out of place. A hand-painted (not original) border of white flamingos near the ceiling has an appropriate aquatic Deco theme.

Chips on the front apron and around the overflow of this pedestal sink can be easily touched up. Turquoise, black, and lavender tile are typical of 1920s bungalows. A tiled-in footed tub such as this one was a lot more common than one would expect.

A height of thirty-six inches (like a kitchen counter) is a much better height for most people. A wall-hung sink can be raised fairly easily, as can a vanity-mounted sink. A pedestal sink will require some sort of plinth.

Early sinks used rubber stoppers on a chain, but versions of pop-up–type stoppers appeared as early as 1893. The sanitarians believed that the chains harbored germs, and favored the pop-up waste fittings, but personally, I think that a plug is much more straightforward and practical, and probably more sanitary as well.

Obsessive Restoration (Sinks)

If you have the original sink, and it is in reasonably good condition, the obvious thing is to keep it. An under-mount sink in a slab that has cracked or become crazed can be replaced with a similar one. Salvage slabs are also available if the slab is damaged (and try to differentiate between damage and patina). There are cleaners and poultices available for stone and marble—once it is clean, it should then be sealed. Cast-iron sinks tend to rust around the overflow holes, but this can be cleaned with rust remover, and possibly touched up with appliance paint. Cast-iron pedestal sinks can also rust at the bottom of the pedestal; depending on how bad it is, it can be cleaned up and touched up. Sinks that are too far gone can be refinished. There are both national franchises and local companies that offer this service. It's basically high-tech paint, so it won't last like porcelain, but most companies give at least a five-year guarantee. Sinks don't get very hard wear, so it can last a lot longer than that, especially if you avoid abrasive cleansers. If the fixture is being refinished in white, use antique white or match the paint to the fixture: bright white won't look right. Many salvage sinks are also available. Self-rimming sinks that sit on top of the counter were not very common (a few were seen in the nineteenth century—descended from the washbasin). These generally look too modern, except in the context of a Victorian bathroom with a washstand-like lavatory.

If the original sink (or other fixtures) is gone, what you do will depend much on the year of the house. It's possible to put in a pretty generic bathroom that could span anywhere from about 1885 to 1930 by using a rolled-rim cast-iron sink, a low-tank toilet, a claw-foot tub, white hexagonal-tile floor, and wooden baseboards. On the other hand, if the other fixtures are lavender and the tile is black and green, you will want to try to find a matching sink (or have one refinished to match everything else). Another option is to get the sink in another wild color such as yellow. In large part, fixtures were white until the late 1920s and 1930s, even if they were in a brightly tiled bathroom.

Another sticky question is whether to take the bathroom back to the year the house was built, if, for instance, the bathroom of a 1902 house was remodeled in the 1930s. In preservation terms, remodels can gain historic stature in their own right, though there is much disagreement on the issue. What year to restore a house to is a serious question, particularly for house museums, and there is no right answer. I would consider it very seriously, and possibly get professional advice, if your house is architecturally significant. In a tract bungalow, on the other hand, it's up to you. If the bathroom is functional and you like it, it's probably easiest to keep it, even if it's not original. On the other hand, I wouldn't hesitate one minute to rip out a bathroom from the 1970s, even though someday it, too, will be historic, and I'll probably be thrown out of preservation for recommending it.

Vanities (with sinks) commonly date to either the nineteenth century or the 1920s and 1930s. (A few may have been seen in the teens). Nineteenth-century ones are based on washstands, and can be

A large rectangular fluted pedestal sink at the 1911 Lanterman House in La Cañada-Flintridge has more space on top than most, but still has a glass shelf above, as well as a cup-and-sponge holder. Above the oblong-tile wainscoting is a mural (awaiting restoration) of water lilies and other aquatic plants.

quite elaborate in prevailing Victorian styles (Rococo, Japonesque, Eastlake, etc.). Later ones tended to be simple cabinets with stone, tile, or wooden tops.

The biggest drawback of many vintage sinks is that there is very little space to put anything down on the countertop. A shelf over the sink is useful in this regard, and often wall-hung or pedestal sinks were flanked by cabinets, providing extra counter space. A table can also be useful for this purpose.

Compromise Solution

Our current demands on bathroom sinks are not that different from the turn of the twentieth century, but center around three things: we want two sinks, we want mixing faucets, and we want counter space. There are many variables in dealing with this. Are you making a brand-new bathroom in a brand-new space, or remodeling one in an existing space? Is

Two pedestal sinks flanking a marble-topped cabinet provide plenty of space for two people, and a continuous shelf above provides even more counter and display space. Dark-stained bead-board wainscoting sets off the white fixtures and black-and-white mosaic-tile floor. Ribbed window glass provides privacy. A large mirror helps this generously sized bath appear even larger.

the existing one original, or are you ripping out something from the 1970s? What year is the house? What are the other bathrooms (if any) like? Is it a big fancy house or a tiny bungalow? (In general, a bigger, fancier house will have a bigger bathroom, though this is by no means universal.)

If there is space, go ahead and put in two sinks—there is certainly precedent for it. If there's not room, perhaps a sink could be added elsewhere, possibly in

the bedroom. Otherwise you may have to make do with one. Mixing faucets are not a problem, although installing one on a sink that previously had separate taps requires a "one-hole" type faucet, and the other hole will have to be capped somehow (a soap dish is often used for this purpose.) Counter space is also fairly easy to come by: "console"-style pedestal sinks have large tops, flanking cabinets or shelving can be installed, or a vanity can be used. Try to avoid the

Console-style sinks provide more counter space, and this one even includes integral chrome towel bars. Mottled green tile with yellow and black accents and a lavender floor is typical of the exuberant tile combinations used in the 1920s and 1930s.

LIQUID ASSETS

"Chippendale never designed a bathtub."

~*Paul Frankl*

favored interior-designer concept of cutting a hole in the top of a dresser or other piece of furniture and using it for a vanity.

There are many fine reproductions of historic sinks available, as well as salvage sinks. Don't use overly modern-looking sinks, such as sculptured pedestals and "vessel" sinks, which are currently very trendy (vessel sinks sit on top of the counter like a bowl). And stay away from the overly cutesy pedestal sinks that are sold at home centers—even the most excessively Victorian sinks were not that twitty. Hand-painted sinks were pretty much a nineteenth-century phenomenon; by the turn of the twentieth century, plain white was dominant. And what to do if you have colored fixtures and you hate them? Get over it. Develop an appreciation for them and the time that they represent. This is easier said than done, but you can learn to love lavender and green.

Early Victorian-era bathtubs made of sheet metal were encased in wood, often elaborately paneled. Copper tubs could be left as is, but tin, zinc, or iron tubs were usually painted inside. The paint didn't hold up very well when exposed to hot water, so these tubs had to be repainted regularly. The first cast-iron tubs were also painted until the process of glazing with porcelain was perfected in the late nineteenth century. Even after that, the outsides were usually painted (as they still are), although it was possible to have the outside glazed as well for a higher price. Victorian tubs frequently had elaborate painted decoration on the outside—swags, floral designs, marbleizing, or even water-themed murals. In the twentieth century, the painting became simplified—a Greek key border or a few gold lines. Solid porcelain tubs were also available, though they were heavier and more expensive.

There were two styles of tubs: the French (slanted on one end) and the Roman (slanted on both ends). The French style was by far the most popular. There were also a few "slipper" tubs, where the rim is higher at the back than at the front. These were what we now call claw-foot tubs, since they often sported decorative ball-and-claw feet. The first ones appeared about 1860, and they continued to be sold well into the 1930s. The cast-iron type generally had a rolled rim, although some had wooden rims. Some Victorian tubs also contained elaborate built-in shower enclosures, ranging from wood-paneled rounded hoods to simpler shower rings with curtains.

Another type of tub meant to be faced with tile on one or more sides was also popular. In 1911, the

Eggplant-colored paint and gold feet dress up this tub set in a bead-board-lined alcove for a new bath in a 1918 bungalow. A wall-mounted cabinet provides storage and a handy shelf, and is stenciled with a lily-of-the-valley motif. The brass plumbing is echoed by brass towel bars and other brass accents, while a vintage Pear's Soap poster adds an appropriate decorative element.

Left: A hand-painted ribbon swag adorns this elaborately footed tub. (Courtesy of Vintage Plumbing.)
Top right: Simple gold striping decorates the outside of a bathtub at the 1901 Stimson-Green Mansion in Seattle.
Bottom right: A Roman tub on a pedestal is shown in this illustration from an early-twentieth-century plumbing catalog.

double-walled cast-iron tub we are familiar with was perfected. It could be fit into a niche or a corner, and solved the problem of trying to clean under and behind a footed bathtub. Although some builders solved this problem by taking a claw-foot tub and plastering it in (this was often an economic decision, as a footed tub was cheaper than the double-wall model), others went so far as to provide a "sunken tub" by cutting a hole in the floor and setting a footed tub in a frame like a modern self-rimming sink, leaving the feet hanging in the basement or crawl space. This was a little dangerous, not to mention cold. Although tubs came in various lengths, eventually the cast-iron five-foot tub in a niche became the standard.

American Standard introduced the Neo-Angle tub in the 1930s (a tub about four feet square, with the tub part angled from corner to corner, leaving places to sit in the other two corners), but it did not gain wide acceptance. Eventually other tub materials were introduced, such as porcelain over steel, fiberglass, acrylic, and porcelain over composite material, but basic tub designs have not changed much. Color came to tubs in the late 1920s, but white is still the preferred color.

As mentioned before, tubs often included showers, partly as a space-saving measure as bathrooms became smaller, but also because a tub makes a pretty good shower receptor. Claw-foot tubs could be fitted up with a round or oval ring to hold the shower curtain(s), and shower plumbing extended up from the tub faucet. A tub in a niche or a corner could have a shower added to one end, and a straight or L-shaped rod accommodated the curtain. Glass doors began to appear after about 1911, though they were not common and were more likely to be found on stall showers rather than tubs. Many of these tubs were surrounded only by lath and plaster even though they included showers, a combination that eventually leads to rot.

In popular culture, tub bathing has been associated with women, both for erotic reasons (a glamorous woman in a bubble bath is a well-known image both in advertising and movies), and because of an unfounded belief that women were somehow too delicate for the "invigorating" shower. This belief has certainly been put to rest, and now showering is the most popular method of cleansing for both sexes. While this may be partly due to being pressed for time, the bath has taken on more of a relaxation role in modern life.

Iridescent blue-and-purple tile with white accents looks quite conservative surrounding an all-porcelain tub in an arched niche in this 1920s home. Lavender ceramic crown molding finishes the top of the wall.

Obsessive Restoration (Bathtubs)

If the existing vintage tub is in good shape, by all means keep it. Often all tubs need is cleaning. One that is too far gone (because of too many years of abrasive scrubbing or the addition of non-slip decals, which eat into the finish) can be refinished. This is basically paint, so it won't hold up like porcelain. Refinishing is also good for changing the color of an otherwise perfectly good tub. (Maybe it's a really hideous color from the 1950s: the worst color tub I ever saw was one I would describe as "yellowish pea-soup green." On the other hand, you could actually run with that, because it's kind of an Arts and Crafts color, and make it into a really earth-tone Arts and Crafts bathroom. More on this under "Decor.") Both national franchises and local companies offer this service. Antique white is best for white fixtures, and colors can also be custom-mixed to match colored fixtures or to change colors. It is also possible to have

A tile-in bathtub set in the center of a large bathroom evokes Hollywood glamour in a 1927 Italian Renaissance–style home. Two cubbyholes set into the tiled platform keep extra towels and bath salts close at hand. Filtered light from etched leaded-glass windows illuminates the room, and a wall of cabinets underneath provides abundant storage for less-glamourous bath items.

weight, fragility, and higher price, means there are far fewer of them. They hold up pretty well, except for minor crazing in the glaze. By the mid-twentieth century, enameled steel was also being used, and by the end of the twentieth century, fiberglass, acrylic, and enameled composite tubs were available. Of these, only enameled composite is really an acceptable substitute for cast iron.

If the tub is being replaced, there are a few things to consider. There weren't any double-wall tubs before 1911, although there were tubs that were meant to be faced with tile. If there's going to be a shower over the tub, it's important that the bottom of the tub be flat enough to stand in (some aren't). Although a footed tub is lovely and often appropriate, it does not provide the best showering experience (it's claustrophobic, the curtain tends to stick to you, water tends to escape). It might be better to provide a separate shower. There is precedent for enclosing footed tubs in a niche—usually surrounded by plaster. This generally leads to rot in the enclosing walls, so I would suggest tiling the inside of the niche. Double-wall tubs were also installed with only a plaster surround; again, I would recommend installing tile. Sometimes the walls are tiled only part way up (two or three feet, or sometimes just one row of tile) around the tub. This is fine if the tub is only used for bathing, and the joint between the tile and the plaster is well caulked. But if a shower is involved, consider adding more tiles, up to a height of five feet or so.

tubs re-porcelained, although this involves removing them and sending them out to be done. The outsides of footed tubs (if originally painted) can be repainted. Oil-based (alkyd) paint is best—latex tends to cause rust. If it's appropriate to the house, decorative painting (striping, marbleizing, stenciling, or murals) can be applied to the outside of a painted tub.

Enameled cast iron is by far the most prevalent tub material. Some all-porcelain tubs were sold, but the difficulty of making them, combined with their

Occasionally tub niches might have been lined with marble or structural glass rather than tile. Tubs come in various lengths, so, depending on space, a shorter or longer one may be in order. A longer one is better for bathing, because you can lie down in it and not have your knees stick out of the water. Installing a replacement double-wall tub also allows insulation to be stuffed in around the tub, which helps keep the bathwater warm. And it may provide an opportunity to add an access door for the plumbing. Another thing to figure out when replacing the tub is how to get the old one out and the new one in. Will it go through the door?

Although tubs sometimes had glass doors, this was the exception rather than the rule. Unlike modern sliding bypass doors, early ones tended to be either a single fixed sheet of glass covering half the length of the tub, or a kind of bi-fold door with leaves. These were framed in metal. The glass was either plate glass or wire glass. These were far more likely to be found in a 1930s bath than an earlier one. Modern equivalents are available: trackless folding doors and fixed sheets of glass. Bypass sliding doors should be avoided—not only are they wrong for a historic bathroom, they're annoying as well. Shower curtains were far more prevalent than doors. Vinyl shower curtains didn't come in until the 1930s; before that shower curtains were either made of duck or white rubber. White rubber is a little hard to come by now, although a "hotel-style" heavy vinyl shower curtain is a fairly good substitute. Duck is still available—it has to be washed periodically to keep it from mildewing. A fabric curtain with a vinyl liner might be an acceptable compromise. Shower curtain rings were metal and are still available.

A high floral border (each flower is made up of six tiles) embellishes a blue tile-in bathtub by Crane set in an arched niche. A coordinating border tops the wainscoting. This Spanish-style house, built in 1932, has five completely unique bathrooms.

Compromise Solution

Bathtubs really haven't changed much except for one development: the whirlpool tub, invented in the 1960s. Now, the whirlpool is a lovely thing—it's relaxing, it eases sore muscles, etc. But I simply cannot bring myself to condone putting one in a historic bathroom. Get a spa and put it in the backyard instead. Or build a separate room for the whirlpool. Something.

Other than that, since many fine salvage and reproduction tubs are available, only space considerations and the other things mentioned under "Obsessive Restoration" will come into play. Tile and possibly marble or structural glass (if appropriate to the age of the bath) are acceptable for lining the walls of a tub niche. Solid surfacing, cultured marble, and acrylic or fiberglass tub surrounds should be avoided. And certainly those all-in-one fiberglass or acrylic tubs with integral surrounds are not appropriate. Glass doors are okay if they're not too modern looking. And have whatever kind of shower curtain you want: iridescent vinyl, tropical fish, fabric, whatever.

LET US SPRAY

Ever since early humans figured out it was refreshing to stand under a waterfall on a hot day, the shower has been a source of invigoration and rejuvenation as well as cleanliness. But it wasn't till the coming of reliable supplies of hot water and the invention of the mixing valve in the late nineteenth century that showers really took off. Before that, for the most part, there were character-building cold showers, usually short; but with the advent of dependable hot water, showers quickly became quite luxurious and complex. Some had up to ten separate controls, allowing the bather to experience a variety of water sensations, either separately or all at once. (Some of these

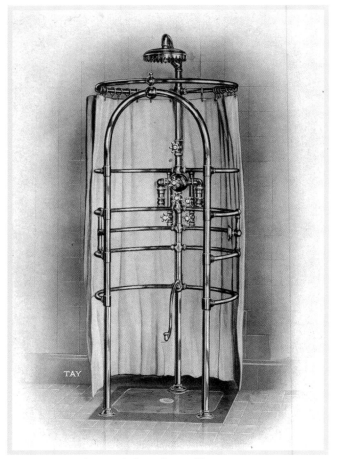

A 1911 cage shower with a white rubber curtain sits over a marble receptor set into the floor. By this time showers were starting to be simplified and contained fewer valves and nozzles.

required sixty gallons per minute in use.) These either were set into paneled hooded cabinets placed over the tub, or used simpler exposed piping. Eventually the wooden paneling was replaced by metal, and around the turn of the twentieth century, separate showers with their own porcelain, tile, terrazzo, or marble receptors had made an appearance. These "cage"-style showers continued in production until the 1920s, either with shower curtains or set into tiled or marble stalls. They came in various shapes, including square, rectangular, round, and space-saving corner models.

In general, showers began to be simplified in the twentieth century, dwindling to fewer and fewer jets,

Nickel-plated pipes and valves are a celebration of the plumber's art in an 1899 shower. An integral thermometer is included, attached to the horizontal mixing tank. The ivory ring is attached to a chain that activates the showerhead.

removing either the tile on the inside or the siding on the outside—easy enough if it was wood siding, rather more difficult for masonry or stucco.

An article in *House and Garden* in the 1920s made the following recommendations for separate shower cabinets:

> There must be a certain pitch to the floor to prevent backing up of water. There should be a lead pan under the receptor about 8" high as to its sides. This prevents any possible seepage of waters through tiling cement. The curb must be high enough and slanted inward so that the water cannot enter the bathroom from the shower, and if there is a door to the cabinet this must be so made that if it opens into a room there is no cartage of water. This is accomplished by a "weep" strip on the edge of the down side and bottom. However, we suggest a curtain and no door. The opening need be but 20", and if your curb, floor, and showerhead are correct, the curtain is ample protection. Doors of tile, plate glass, etc., are handsome, but need constant cleaning.

and finally to a single showerhead. The pipes began to be enclosed in the wall. Separate stall showers (usually tiled) became common, even in smaller bathrooms, although the shower-over-tub combination remained the most popular installation. A tiled shower usually had a shower pan lined with either lead or several layers of hot-mopped asphalt and tar paper (like a tar and gravel roof). These membranes extended up the sidewalls for a few inches. Modern shower pans use a synthetic rubber membrane instead. This was followed by a layer of mortar, sloped to allow for drainage, and then the tile. Small mosaic tiles were usually employed to conform to the slope. Often these were laid in decorative patterns, although plain tiles were also used. It was recommended when enclosing the pipes that the shower be positioned so that an access hatch or panel could be placed in an adjacent closet or other space for access to the pipes. But as homes began to be built more hastily, this advice was often ignored, and pipes were often placed in outside walls with no way to access them short of

A tiled corner shower stall saves space in a small 1929 apartment bathroom. Yellow-and-green tile sets off the green fixtures. Ribbed glass was a common material for shower doors.

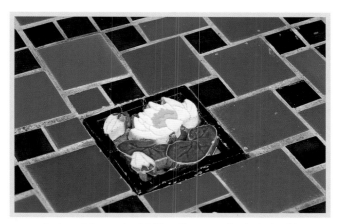

A pierced decorative Malibu tile covers the drain in this shower stall in a modest 1929 Spanish Revival bungalow, but it can be easily removed for cleaning.

The article goes on to say, "For those who want every known convenience, there are on the market anti-scalding devices which make the water mixing device pretty sure, regardless of water pressure." These are similar to modern pressure-balancing anti-scald valves, though the technology has been improved. And a final piece of advice, which we could still take to heart: "Remember that you are often urged to buy 'highfalutin' things which are sometimes excellent

and sometimes rubbish. Be careful. Keep the bathrooms simple. Dispense with what is dispensable and get what is comfortable, studying economy when possible."

Many showers were designed to prevent getting the hair wet. Even in 1929, an advertisement by the Cleanliness Institute advised women to shampoo their hair every two weeks, which was considered frequent at the time. This led to some showerheads being set at a height about five feet off the floor.

This causes contortions in modern humans trying to actually get their hair wet. Six and a half feet from the floor is the recommended height. Various adjustable-height showerheads are also available, allowing users of different heights to be comfortable. Hand-held showers are another option. On the other hand, sunflower-style showerheads, which hang horizontally, are guaranteed to get your hair wet, whether you want to or not.

CURTAINS FOR YOU

Originally shower curtains were made of white rubber. This was replaced by duck (a light cotton canvas) in the early twentieth century. Crane advertised their "Triple Pleat" duck curtains, which had three tucks running along the bottom, allowing for lengthening as they shrunk. Other fabrics such as rubberized taffeta were also tried. This was all there was until 1928, when Waldo Semon, a chemist at B. F. Goodrich, invented polyvinyl chloride (PVC). In the aftermath of the stock market crash in 1929, no one was very interested in uses for this new plastic. But Mr. Semon kept looking for applications, and after watching his wife make curtains, he realized vinyl could be used as a fabric. He gradually won over his superiors, and by the early 1930s, the company was marketing the material under the name Koroseal and using it for shower curtains, umbrellas, and raincoats. He received a patent in 1933. Today PVC is second only to polyethylene as the world's most widely used plastic. Most shower curtains are still made of PVC, although duck is still available, as well as various

Water plants and a swan are etched on the glass shower door in the master bathroom of a 1932 Spanish Revival house. The arch of the shower echoes the vaulted ceiling. Green tile with an elaborate border frames green fixtures and tile-topped storage cabinets.

synthetic fabrics. Glass doors were also used on both showers and tubs, even in the nineteenth century (though this was rare). Glass doors were more prevalent in the 1920s and '30s, particularly on showers. These were made of plate glass or wire glass (a little safer than plate), framed in metal. Modern glass doors are made of safety glass. Many of these glass doors were etched with designs, sometimes aquatic in theme (herons, flamingos) but not always. Sometimes various sorts of obscure glass were used: pebbled, ribbed, etc. As mentioned above, doors require more cleaning than a curtain. Doors on a tub are particularly problematic, even with the introduction of new "trackless" doors. Showers with glass on three sides are rare.

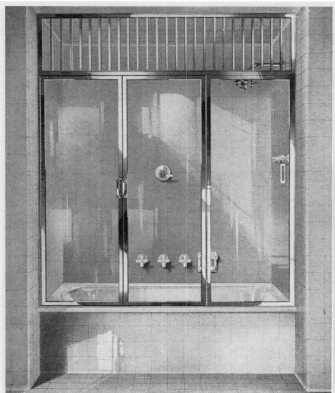

Left: Two glass doors (on the left) open to allow access to this shower-over-tub combination, while the right-hand door is fixed in place. The showerhead is barely visible behind the ventilation grille at the top. Courtesy of Crane Plumbing.

Luckily, the shower pan of this Malibu tiled shower is still intact. If it needed to be re-done, black tile would be the best bet.

Obsessive Restoration (Showers)

In a stall shower, the first thing to fail is the pan. Even with a vitreous china or enameled cast-iron receptor, there may still be leakage around the drain or from the plumbing inside the wall. That's usually the case with a tile receptor as well, although water can also make its way through the grout and mortar. Contrary to popular belief, cement-based products are not waterproof. (More about this under "Tile.") If you're lucky, you'll find out it's leaking before it destroys the ceiling below it. Leakage can lead to rot in the wood supporting the shower. A leaking drain in a china or cast-iron receptor can be replaced, but a leak in a tiled shower pan will leave you no choice but to rip out the pan and at least the bottom two rows of wall tile as well. To do this without destroying the rest of the wall tile is a job best left to a professional. A new membrane and mortar bed can be installed (this is not really a do-it-yourself job), or there is also a pre-formed, ready-to-tile shower pan that can be purchased from a company called Tile-Redi. No matter how obsessive you are, I would not go back to lead or hot mopping for the shower pan.

Then the problem becomes an aesthetic one—since finding a match for the wall or floor tile is unlikely (even white is hard to match, let alone some weird 1920s color), you don't want it to look like a patch job. There are several options, but the main thing that's important is to make it look like it was done on purpose at the time the house was built. For that reason, don't use white in a colored shower. Try black, or a contrasting but complementary color. If the

A re-done shower pan in white hexagonal tile, though not the best choice for a colored tile bath, is set off from the green wall tile by a thin black feature strip.

shower is white, make sure the white replacement tile matches pretty well. You'd be amazed how many shades of white there are. You may be able to match the tile (even colored tile) in color, but often old tile has variations in the glaze that modern mass-produced tile doesn't have. Or it might be close but no cigar—in which case, separating it from the old tile with a feature strip or decorative border will help. You can also try to duplicate the pattern of a decorative mosaic tile floor, or make up a new pattern (some tile companies will do this custom and put it on a backing mesh for you). There are also companies that will do custom glazes, though this is expensive. Another option for replacement pans is terrazzo (marble or stone chips embedded in a cement base and polished). To my knowledge, porcelain and cast-iron receptors are no longer being made, so salvage will be the only option. It is also possible to get a custom receptor made from marble, slate, or other stone. This should have a honed rather than polished finish or it will be too slippery. Occasionally the walls of a stall shower were lined with stone slabs, usually marble—these may need to be removed for the repair, again, a job best left to professionals.

A shower over a tub can have similar problems. A leaking tub drain can usually be repaired from below (although this may involve opening up a ceiling), but a plumbing leak inside the wall, or water penetration through tile or other surface materials, is also common. If leaking pipes are inside the wall, and there is no access panel, it may be necessary to remove wall tiles or panels in order to get to them. If it's remotely possible to get to the pipes from the back and avoid taking out tile, try to use that method. It's much easier to patch plaster, stucco, or wood than it is to remove tile in intact pieces. It is difficult (though not impossible) to remove wall tiles intact, especially because the thin grout lines usual in bathroom tile installations don't allow much room to maneuver.

Best left to professionals, it involves mini-grinders, dental drill bits, a lot of patience, and a backup plan if you fail.

But here's how to go about it, just in case: Mask off adjacent tiles with metal flat-bar stock and duct tape. An assistant with a spray bottle will help to prolong the life of the drill bits, which tend to get red-hot and then break in about thirty seconds—water will extend their life to about two minutes. First, cut along the grout lines with a diamond blade in a mini-grinder. Then use the dental bits to remove the rest of the grout. Now for the tricky part: getting behind the tile. A flexible shaft for the drill bit will help. Usually the best place to start is the hole around the pipe stub-out, because you can get a slightly better angle. The idea is to drill out enough of the area behind the tile that it will come off. This is not easy, especially on the first one. Once the first one is off, it will be easier to get leverage on the others. If you succeed in removing them, it will probably be necessary to patch the mortar behind them after the plumbing is repaired. When re-installing the tile, use big globs of silicone caulk instead of thin-set mortar—it will make the job easier for whoever might need to do it again eighty years hence. On the other hand, if the tile is to be removed and replaced with something else, it will be easier to remove if it is first cut corner to corner with the grinder (cut through the grout first, though). The resulting triangles will be easier to pop off. If water penetration has caused rot in the other walls, it may be necessary to remove all of the tile or panels. If some or all of the tile has to be replaced, the same rules mostly apply as for stall showers. It's best to do something that looks like a decorative panel inset that was done on purpose. If the tub shower is surrounded by plaster, it would be best to replace it with tile, unless you either have a house museum or never take showers.

A waterfall mural framed within a recessed Moorish-style niche and other complex tiling surround a raised lavender tub in a 1929 Spanish-style house. Two pierced tiles for ventilation flank a ceiling-mounted light fixture. Any fixture mounted over a tub or shower should be UL listed for wet areas.

Footed tubs that don't have showers can be converted with the addition of readily available conversion plumbing and a ring to hold the curtain. It's probably a better showering experience in a separate stall shower, but that may not be possible in all cases.

Sometimes there is a window in a stall shower or over the tub. This practically guarantees rot in a wooden window. A window like this should obsessively be kept caulked and sealed, and the addition of a vinyl window curtain over it should be considered.

The restoration of cage showers presents unique challenges. Often the needle-spray tubes are bent or dented and need to be fixed or replaced. Sometimes they need to be reattached to the upright stanchions. Parts may need replating. The valve stems usually need repair or replacement, and often missing handles need to be replaced (not always easy because valve stems are not standardized and vary by manufacturer.) Showerheads may also need replacement or repair. Antique plumbing dealers may be able to do this for you.

Some stall showers had glass doors, and rarely, a tub did also. Broken glass is easily replaced, and metal frames (usually nickel until the 1930s, when chromium plating came in) can be replated if necessary. New glass can also be etched or sandblasted with a design, which can be copied from the existing door (if there is one). A new door should have a metal frame also—frameless doors are a late-twentieth-century invention. Shower curtains for stall showers are a little hard to come by—a bathtub-sized shower curtain is usually 72 by 72 inches, but can be easily cut down to size. A shower over a footed tub will generally require two curtains (although extra-large 168-by-70-inch curtains are available).

It was probably sometime in the 1930s that lighting started to be installed in shower stalls or over tubs. Usually it was recessed in the ceiling using a special waterproof fixture. I will relax my adamant opposition to recessed down lights in this case. You're not allowed to put them anywhere else, though, unless there were already some there.

Grab bars for safety have been sold and recommended since the 1910s. Usually they were ceramic, kind of like vertically installed towel bars. Recessed soap dishes also had grab bars included. None of these would meet modern ADA (Americans with Disabilities Act) requirements, but they're better than nothing. Most modern grab bars are too contemporary looking, but a few that are a little more historic looking are starting to be made. They are a good idea, and especially if you have the walls open for any reason, it's good to install blocking between the studs for attaching them. Special wall fasteners are also available for them if there's no blocking.

Compromise Solution

With so many fine salvage and reproduction fixtures available, most compromises may have more to do with space or lifestyle issues. For instance, modern shower enclosures tend to be large, sometimes with built-in benches and other amenities, while period shower stalls can be quite small. Or perhaps showering in a footed tub with a curtain ring is not your idea of a good time, but there is no room for a separate shower—it may be necessary to replace the footed tub with a tub in a niche. On the other hand, a huge "vertical whirlpool" shower with wraparound glass doors will look decidedly too modern, although the same shower experience could be achieved in a cage shower or a shower with multiple heads. In general, if you are going to install contemporary fixtures, for budget or other reasons, try to stick to fixtures that are fairly plain and unassuming rather than slickly contemporary.

Vintage-style tubs as well as contemporary shower receptors are made in acrylic. These are less expensive and lighter in weight (and for shower receptors, pretty much the only game in town, except for fiberglass). They are plastic, however, and they look it. It is also possible to purchase fully molded shower stalls, as well as tubs with built-in surrounds, made of either acrylic or fiberglass. Don't use them—they're tacky. An acrylic or fiberglass shower receptor with tile walls is an acceptable compromise. Lining tub niches or shower stalls with solid surfacing materials, cultured marble (especially the kind that resembles saltwater taffy—it is neither marble nor cultured), or fiberboard paneling made to look like ceramic tile should be avoided.

Glass doors are okay, but it's best if they have metal frames like old ones. Either clear or obscure glass will work. Shower curtains are easier to clean and come in a wide variety of styles, from tropical fish to neoclassical. Go with whatever floats your boat. Grab bars are a good idea, but at least get the metal kind rather than the plastic.

Mr. Turd's Wild Ride

In Zen Buddhism there is a special ceremony before using the toilet—this verse is to be recited three times:

Adoration to all the Buddhas.

Adoration to all the limitless teaching.

Peace! Speak! Blaze! Up! Open!

To the glorious, peaceful one

For whom there is no disaster

whilst upon the water-closet, Hail!

A toilet with a pillbox-shaped tank and a wooden seat has been placed in a separate tiled room with a terrazzo (marble chips in cement) floor in a grand 1906 Arts and Crafts house. Separating the toilet from the rest of the bathroom is a practical solution that is seeing resurgent popularity in new homes.

The word "toilet" comes from the French word *toile*, meaning linen, and refers originally to a small towel draped around the neck while shaving (in modern usage, *toile* usually refers to toile de Jouy: fabric printed with an eighteenth-century French scenic pattern in one color on a light ground). Toilet (*toilette* in French) also refers to the act of dressing or washing, but primarily it refers to the fixture. There are, of course, many euphemisms employed as well. As detailed previously, a series of inventions and improvements over the last several centuries has brought us to the modern siphon-jet toilet, which was pretty much in place by the turn of the twentieth century, although wash-down, wash-out, and even hopper closets continued to be sold. (Hopper closets were still in catalogs as late as 1926.) There were also hybrid-action wash-down closets. But the siphon-jet

Although a flush lever is the most common mechanism, push buttons like this one, as well as pull chains and emergency brake–type levers, were also used to activate the flushing mechanism. This commode is in the 1906 DeForest House by Greene and Greene.

Simple embossed beading decorates a wash-down bowl at the DeForest House. It is attached to the wood floor with the typical four bolts. The two in back connect to the flange of the drain, while the two in front fasten directly into the wood floor.

toilet won the day and continues to be used, with a few modifications for low-flow water saving.

High-tank toilets were more prevalent in the nineteenth century, though low tanks were available even then. High tanks use gravity to advantage and thus save water, using an average of two or three gallons per flush. On the other hand, they are quite noisy. In the twentieth century, although high tanks continued to be sold, the low tank was far more prevalent. These hung on the wall and connected to the bowl with an L-shaped pipe. (In modern two-piece toilets, the tank sits directly on the bowl.) The low tank allowed them to be placed under windows or stairways or other places where a high tank wouldn't fit. Tanks were originally made from wood lined with copper or lead; vitreous china tanks were questioned as to their strength when first introduced, leading the Eljer Company to stage a demonstration in which twenty-seven men stood on a plank balanced on a vit-

reous tank, which remained intact. Most tanks were rectangular, although the fronts could be curved, and round "pillbox" tanks were also manufactured. Although the push-down handle we are familiar with was common, toilets also flushed with push buttons, pull-up buttons, pull-up handles (usually located at the bottom of the tank), or in the case of high-tank toilets, a pull chain.

The bowls varied in shape according to whether they were siphon-jet or wash-down. A wash-down (or the hybrid siphonic-action wash-down) bowl usually has a bulge in the front, a slope inside, and a fairly small water area. A siphon-jet bowl has a larger water area and resembles a bowl on a pedestal. Both kinds are oval in shape, although in modern parlance these are known as "round," and bowls that are even more oval are known as "elongated." Various methods were tried for attaching the bowl to the drain, from screw-type joints to various kinds of flanges. These varied

An unusual teardrop-shaped seat with nickel-plated hinges is featured on a siphon-jet toilet in the 1908 Gamble House. Two-inch white hexagonal tile on the floor and white-tile wainscoting are typical of early-twentieth-century "sanitary" bathrooms.

become a problem for the elderly and disabled, who find it difficult to get up and down off a lower toilet.

Colored toilets were introduced in the late 1920s with the advent of colored porcelain, but as with the other fixtures, the most popular color for toilets was, and remains, white. Black was introduced in the 1930s and is still available, along with other colors, but there is something really scary about a black toilet. Of course, you never have to clean it, because how can you tell if it's dirty? Still, lavender, green, yellow, or some other color fixtures in a wildly colored tiled space are one of the great delights of 1920s and '30s bathrooms.

Toilet seats in the nineteenth century were made of varnished wood (usually oak, mahogany, or pine), and these continued to be available in the twentieth century as well. The concern with sanitation led to the adoption of white-painted wooden seats as the only "sanitary" solution. Advertisements for Church Seats trumpeted, "Would you like to transform your bathroom in ten minutes? A new Church Sani-White Seat, a completely modern, sanitary seat, is very moderate in cost. It can be attached in ten minutes to any bowl with an ordinary pair of pliers." When colored toilets came in, seats were painted to match, or black was sometimes used. Some seats at this time were also made of hard rubber. Seats continue to be made of wood, although various plastics and even padded vinyl are also sold.

Recent code changes now require 1.6 gallons-per-flush toilet. Many old toilets use six or seven gallons per flush. This can be cut down somewhat with dams in the tank and such, but particularly with the wash-down types, a certain amount of water is needed for a proper flush. The early low-flow toilet models were less than satisfactory, often clogging or requiring repeated flushing. But recent models have been greatly improved.

from manufacturer to manufacturer. Some toilets had a ceramic horn on the bottom that fit down inside the drain or flange (particularly useful with a lead closet bend and no flange), while others bolted to a flange attached to the drain and also to the floor. Modern toilets bolt to a flange with two bolts, while old toilets generally had four bolts: two for the flange, and two that bolted into the floor. The joint was (and still is) sealed with a thick wax ring to keep water from leaking out. Some manufacturers also offered a porcelain or marble plate for the toilet to be set on, which could be set into the floor. Toilet bowls have been getting progressively lower over the years: old toilets average about sixteen inches high, where a modern toilet is about fourteen inches high. This has increasingly

Obsessive Restoration (Toilets)

There is a definite ecological quandary involved when it comes to toilet restoration. Should you replace the existing vintage toilet, which may use 6 or 7 gallons per flush, with a new 1.6-gallon toilet, even though that will mean the old toilet will go to the landfill where it will certainly not biodegrade? (Archaeologists don't call them potsherds for nothing—ceramics last pretty much forever.) It's a difficult decision. Although discarded tubs and sinks can have a new life—either at the salvage yard or as birdbaths, planters, or horse troughs—toilets are not popular for these uses, probably because of their original function, although one would think with the fertilizer connection. . . .

If you're redoing the whole bathroom with permits, code requirements may decide the question for you. Otherwise, I tend to come down on the side of keeping the old toilet and saving water elsewhere by using strategies such as installing a low-flow showerhead, buying a water-saving washing machine and dishwasher, replacing irrigation-requiring landscape plants with drought-tolerant varieties, etc. Some water can be saved by installing toilet dams or otherwise retrofitting the tank mechanism. Some other reasons to replace an existing vintage toilet include serious cracks in the tank or bowl (as opposed to crazing in the glaze, which is mainly cosmetic).

The operation of a toilet is fairly simple. When the

Apartment buildings often use pressure flush valves like this one, rather than tanks, because they save water. This bowl has an extended "sanitary" lip, and is part of a colorfully tiled 1929 bath in an Art Deco building. A built-in ceramic tissue holder is installed to the left of the sink, and accessories such as a round blue-glass mirror and an antique step-on trash receptacle add to the vintage look.

flush handle is pushed (or pulled or whatever), a trip lever lifts the tank ball or flapper, opening the tank outlet and allowing water to flow into the bowl. This causes the contents of the bowl to be siphoned through the trap and into the drain. (It is possible to flush a toilet simply by dumping a bucket of water directly into the bowl.) When the tank is nearly empty, the tank ball or flapper falls back into place over the outlet. The float or ball cock falls with the water level in the tank, opening the water-supply inlet valve just as the outlet closes. The tank is refilled through the filler tube. At the same time, water refills the bowl through the overflow pipe. As the water level in the tank nears the top of the overflow pipe, the float rises and closes the inlet valve.

Another mechanism used is called a pressure

Though most toilet tanks were rectangular, some were rounded in front, pillbox-shaped, or even wavy like this one, shown on a siphon-jet toilet in a 1911 plumbing catalog.

or broken, it is possible to replace these separately with salvaged ones. Just make sure they are stylistically compatible. For the bowl in particular, if the replacement bowl has a horn on the bottom that fits down inside the flange, make sure your drain is the right size—a four-inch horn will not fit into a three-inch drain.

The parts inside the tank are fairly standardized and easy to replace. (Consult a plumbing book for how-tos.) Wooden tanks lined with metal may leak and will have to be either re-lined or replaced. Leakage may also have damaged the wood beyond repair. It's probably a good idea to replace a lead-lined tank anyway. (Be sure to dispose of it at a hazardous-waste facility.) A salvaged wood tank will be harder to find than a ceramic one, although reproductions are being made. Another problem with tanks is condensation: since the tank is full of cold water, on a hot day in a humid climate, water will condense on the tank and drip onto the floor. The tank can be lined with waterproof insulation to help with this problem. And just in case you want that Victorian hand-painted look in your toilet bowl, there is a company making decals for this purpose (see "Resources").

Many toilets have a date of manufacture stamped inside the lid or the tank. This date may be a year or two before the toilet was actually installed, since it may have been sitting around a warehouse. Take this date with a grain of salt, since it's also possible that either the lid or the toilet was replaced at some point. It can also tell you approximately what year the bathroom was remodeled, if the bath is obviously more recent than the house.

Reproductions of high-tank toilets are also being made. Unfortunately, no reproductions of low-tank toilets with flush elbows are currently being produced. There are old-looking toilets, but the tank sits directly on the bowl, which makes them look modern. These meet the 1.6-gallon flush requirement. Most of

flush valve. Usually found in apartment buildings or public restrooms, these mechanisms eliminate the tank and save water but are noisy. Lack of a visible tank does not necessarily mean that there isn't one. Sometimes the tank is concealed inside the wall (hopefully with some kind of access to it).

If the existing toilet is going to be kept, here are a few problems you might encounter. Usually the first thing to go on a toilet is the tank lid (probably because somebody dropped it). If you still have the lid, take it with you to the salvage yard to look for a replacement. Lids are not standardized because tanks are not standardized. If it's a colored lid, the selection will be smaller, and you may be out of luck. If the lid is missing, make a template of the tank top and take that to the salvage yard. If the tank or bowl is cracked these are white, so a colored one will be harder to come by. Make sure the rough-in (the distance from the wall behind the toilet to the center of the drain) matches: modern toilets generally have a twelve-inch rough-in, whereas older toilets usually had a fourteen-inch. Measure to be sure, since this was never really standardized. The same holds true with salvage toilets—make sure the rough-in matches. And after removing the old toilet, make sure the floor hasn't rotted and that there's a flange attached to the drain. Well up into the 1920s, toilets were being installed with only a lead closet bend and no flange. It's a good idea to replace a lead closet bend. Old toilet tanks were made to be mounted on the wall, unlike modern toilets, which are freestanding. If a high-tank toilet is replacing a low one (or vice versa), it may be necessary to install blocking in the wall so the tank can be bolted to solid wood, depending whether the holes in the tank fall on a stud location.

Toilet bowls are either "round" (kind of oval) or "elongated" (really oval). Elongated bowls take up more space, which may be an issue, but primarily it's an aesthetic decision. An elongated bowl is ostensibly more sanitary.

It's important to know which you have, though, if you have to replace the seat. Many kinds of seats are available, including painted and unpainted wood, plastic, and padded vinyl. Only wood is really appropriate for an old toilet. A colored toilet may be difficult to match—in that case, either a contrasting but compatible color, or black, is best. White tends to stand out too much on a colored toilet.

Compromise Solution

If your solution to the ecological dilemma is to install a modern 1.6-gallon toilet, here are a few things to keep in mind. In a reproduction of an old toilet, all the things stated above will apply (matching rough-in, etc.). Reproduction high-tank toilets cost more than a home-center toilet, so budget constraints may come into play. Old-looking low-tank toilets still look fairly modern because the tank sits directly on the bowl rather than hanging on the wall. If your budget calls for a modern toilet from the home center instead of a reproduction, get one with a rectangular tank rather than a tank that is tapered toward the bottom, as these look too modern; get a two-piece toilet (a one-piece toilet, with the toilet and tank all in one and usually a very low profile, would only be appropriate for a 1940s or '50s bath); be aware that modern toilets usually have a twelve-inch rough-in (if the old rough-in was fourteen inches, the new toilet will be two or three inches from the wall); check the trap (stick your hand in it—the bigger and smoother it is the better). A toilet with a non-standard rough-in will probably have to be special ordered. Some 1.6-gallon toilets have special inner workings to make them flush better, like compressed air. In general, the less-expensive toilets don't work as well, with a few exceptions. If a modern toilet is being installed in a bath where the other fixtures are colored, avoid white. If you can't match the existing fixtures, try to find a toilet in a compatible color, or else use black. In general, try to avoid really modern-looking or sculptural toilets, and stick with something fairly plain.

There are also other kinds of toilets available for special situations such as basements (toilets that flush up), or rural areas where sewers or septic tanks aren't available. A modern version of the earth closet, called a composting toilet, is sold by various manufacturers. Another option is a toilet that uses flames (natural gas or propane) to incinerate the waste. One brand name for these is Incinolet, though my personal favorite, which was in a cabin my sister lived in, was called the Destroylet. One great advantage of these is that, on a cold winter morning, they can be "flushed" first to warm up the seat.

Here Bidet, Gone Tomorrow (Other Fixtures)

Bidets have never been widely used in the U.S., probably because of our basic discomfort with their purpose. Many people don't even know what they are. While they can be useful for many purposes, such as washing your feet or chilling extra drinks at parties, their primary function is to cleanse the genital area of either sex. Shaped similar to toilets, they are plumbed for hot and cold water, and have an upward spraying device in the bowl. While there are other ways to cleanse these parts of the body (a handheld shower works well), only a bidet allows you to do it without taking all your clothes off. They take up as much space as a toilet, though, which is why it's unlikely one would have been installed in a small bungalow, and they are not very common even in larger, fancier houses.

Foot and/or sitz baths were a little more popular, though mostly confined to larger bathrooms in grander houses. Footbaths were supposed to be used for soaking the feet, but plenty of them were also pressed into service for washing babies and dogs. Sitz or hip baths were meant to be sat in, and therefore were lower in the front. Although a sitz bath could accomplish the same cleansing as a bidet, they were used more to treat conditions for which we now have medications (think hemorrhoids), or in situations where full bathing wasn't possible, such as having one's leg in a cast. And, of course, for washing small children and dogs. They were made in both enameled cast iron and solid porcelain. If foot or sitz baths were installed, it was usually one or the other, not both. They were mostly discontinued by the 1930s.

Obsessive Restoration (Other Fixtures)

If you have any of these fixtures, you might as well keep them. As with tubs and sinks, they can be refinished if necessary, although they probably were not subject to such hard wear that this will be required. If you want to add these kinds of fixtures, you will need the space to do so. To my knowledge, they are not being reproduced (except for bidets, which are still being made), so salvaged ones will have to be used. These may also require antique fittings, which will be harder to come by than the average reproduction faucet.

Right: An illustration from the 1911 American Standard catalog shows a bath with a full complement of fixtures, including a foot bath, wall-hung sink, claw-foot tub, and, in an adjoining room, a wash-down toilet with a wooden tank. The charming drawing at the bottom illustrates a favored use for foot and sitz baths—bathing small children and dogs.

DESIGN NUMBER P 25

ALL TAPPED OUT

"Time heals all things, except a leaky faucet."

~*Sam Ewing*

Fuller ball valve faucet

Compression faucet

Once there is water flowing through a pipe, a way to stop and start the flow at will is required. Thus the faucet was invented. Ancient ones were fairly primitive, akin to the tap on a beer keg. In the nine-teenth century, faucets were the subject of much experimentation, as with all plumbing. Eventually two types of faucet mechanisms won the day: the Fuller ball valve and the compression faucet. The Fuller-type valves were the first popular faucets, but they died out after the 1920s because they required more maintenance. Compression faucets became the universal faucet type, as they still are.

Fuller ball valves feature a lever handle attached to a stem, which is offset or bent, rather like a crank-shaft. When the lever is rotated, a conical soft rubber disc (the ball) moves either against or away from a metal seat, controlling the flow of water. Only a half turn of the lever was required to open or close the faucet. Fuller ball valves continued to be sold well into the 1920s.

By the 1890s, more sophisticated compression faucets came into use. Though more complex to man-ufacture, they were easier to maintain and allowed a more variable water flow. In a compression valve, a cross or lever handle controls a stem, which is threaded down into the body of the valve. When the stem is rotated by turning the handle, it moves a hard rubber disc either against or away from a metal seat, which closes or opens an orifice in the valve body, controlling the water flow. This basic design is still used in faucets today. Modern improvements include the use of ceramic disc cartridges in place of the rubber washer.

Initially both these types of faucets started out as separate taps for hot and cold, but mixing faucets, which mixed the two, were a necessity for showers and bathtubs, and that use was quite common by the late nineteenth century. For some reason, mixing faucets didn't become common on sinks until the 1930s, probably because people continued to use their sinks like washbasins, filling them with water for shaving or washing rather than using running water, which is still a good water-saving idea. Both Fuller and compression-style mixing faucets were available.

Top: Wall-mounted handles operate a spout that is molded into the lip of a 1929 pedestal sink. A ceramic tissue holder is mounted nearby.
Middle: Brass gooseneck tub faucets on a claw-foot bathtub look good and also solve a modern code problem: the spout cannot be lower than the overflow.
Bottom: A square Deco faucet with green porcelain handles matches the green pedestal sink in a 1930s remodel of a 1914 bathroom.

Mixing valves for showers could be had with anti-scald or pressure-balancing devices, not unlike those of today. Showers over tubs often had separate faucets from the ones servicing the tub.

Most faucets were pretty simple in shape, although in the 1930s stylized Art Deco–influenced faucets were designed, and the very wealthy always had access to elaborate faucets with chased designs, fancy handles, and spouts in the shape of fish or lions and such. But plain faucets were the most common.

Although low spouts were frequently used, gooseneck spouts were also used, as the height was useful (on both sinks and tubs) for hair washing. Some 1920s and '30s sinks had an integral porcelain spout molded into the sink. Many tub spouts were narrow and ribbed so that a rubber hose for a handheld shower spray could be attached. Some tub spouts were also made of porcelain.

In the nineteenth century, faucet handles were generally made of metal, but by the turn of the twentieth century, porcelain handles had come into vogue, probably because they were white and "sanitary," although metal handles continued to be used. Fuller ball faucets always had lever handles, but compression faucets could have either cross handles or lever handles. Typical cross handles had four arms, but a five-arm "star" handle was also available. Either the handle or a button on the faucet was labeled "hot" or "cold" (or "H" and "C"), although the hot water was traditionally on the left, and still is.

Bronze and brass have always been the favored materials for faucet bodies. Most modern faucets are made of brass. Plain brass was a common faucet finish in the nineteenth century and into the twentieth, but it requires a lot of polishing to keep it shiny. Nickel plating mostly solved that problem and was a favored option for faucets from the 1880s until it was almost entirely replaced by chromium (chrome) plating in the 1930s. It is interesting to note that brass must still be plated with nickel first before it can be plated with chrome, because chrome will stick to nickel but it won't stick to brass. The very wealthy, of course, could also have gold or silver plating on their faucets.

Showerheads ranged from the very large "rain shower" style (now known as "sunflower" shower-heads) to smaller rosette-style heads. As the twentieth century progressed, showerheads became smaller and very much resemble those in use today. Showerheads were generally metal (brass or plated brass), although heads in which the spray part was made of porcelain were also fairly common. The "telephone" shower, where a handheld shower rests in a horizontal cradle, was a regular fixture on footed tubs. The handheld shower was sometimes a feature of stall showers or showers over tubs as well.

Obsessive Restoration (Faucets)

The main problem with old faucets is leaking. Often this can fixed with simple washer replacement, although sometimes the valve seat (which the washer presses against when the faucet is closed) is no longer smooth and needs to be ground down a little. There is a special tool for this, called, not surprisingly, a valve-seat grinder. A useful resource in all this will be a plumbing-supply house or hardware store that has been in business for a long time and still has archaic parts lying around. But sometimes a faucet is just too far gone to be rebuilt. Luckily, there are many fine reproductions being made, both with separate hot and cold taps and mixing faucets. It is possible to replace single taps with a mixing faucet, depending on how far apart the holes are. Modern faucets are made for holes either four or eight inches apart (often referred to as "widespread"). Some widespread faucets require three holes, one for each handle and one for the spout—these can spread up to twelve inches. It is possible to drill an extra hole, but this is not a do-it-your-

Top: This 1906 sink originally had a mixing faucet (spout in center) that was disconnected, with the spout left in place. The original handles were removed and replaced with separate taps. It has since been restored to its original configuration. Bottom: Kits were available to turn separate taps into mixing faucets, as shown here on a 1932 bathtub.

self job. Another option is a "one-hole" faucet, but this will require plugging the other hole with either some sort of escutcheon or a soap dish.

Reproductions of Fuller-type faucets are also available. It's important to make sure the spout of a sink faucet is long enough to reach over the edge of the basin. Reproduction faucets are once again start-ing to be plated with nickel, and that is usually the best choice unless the bathroom dates from the 1930s or later. The plating has often worn off old faucets, particularly on the handles. Although they are perfectly functional this way, and you can learn to love patina, they can also be replated. Sink faucets, by the way, were almost always deck-mounted rather than wall-mounted, except for a few that were wall-mounted on a high backsplash.

Faucets may have undergone handle replacement at some point. If the replacement handle is inappropriate, it can be replaced with something more appropriate. If you know the manufacturer of the faucet (unlikely, but one could get lucky), it will be easier to find a replacement handle. If not, be sure to take either the whole faucet or at least the valve stem when looking for a replacement handle. Valve stems are not standardized and vary with the manufacturer. It may actually be easier to get a replacement faucet, either new or salvage, than to find a replacement handle that fits. There are plastic adapters for sale that ostensibly adjust to any valve stem, but these tend to strip rather quickly, so they are only a short-term solution.

The rules apply to both shower and tub faucets, except for some code issues. The building code in most areas requires an anti-scald valve on the shower. Whether a vintage anti-scald valve will meet code may be up to the inspector. If not, reproductions are available. Usually an anti-scald valve will have one handle, which should be a porcelain or metal cross or lever. Another option is to install a different type of anti-scald valve that can be attached to the supply pipes at a point before the shower—this has to be accessible through a panel or in the basement or crawl space—or it can be attached right near the water heater. Another code issue is that many old tub faucets (as well as some reproductions) have their spouts below what is called the "flood rim" (where the overflow plate is); this can allow backflow of tub water into the supply lines, possibly contaminating the supply. An existing tub faucet is ordinarily "grandfathered" in, but if it is being replaced, there may be problems with the building inspector. A gooseneck tub faucet could be a solution. Showers over tubs usually were served by faucets independent of the tub faucets, as opposed to the modern practice of having one set of faucets for both with a diverter to send water to one or the other, although vintage diverters are not unheard of.

Modern faucet sets, whether for sinks, showers, or tubs, generally include a waste-and-overflow with a pop-up drain. Although pop-up drains were an option even in the nineteenth century, a drain with a rubber plug was far more common, and it is still possible to purchase that sort of waste-and-overflow.

Supply lines used to be made of plated soft copper tubing, which can still be obtained. Modern plastic supply lines should only be used where they can't be seen. Shut-off valves (also known as angle stops) used to have cross or star handles, as opposed to the oval wheel handles that are currently used. Existing ones should be used if they still work.

Compromise Solution

There is very little need to compromise on faucets, unless you just can't live without a shower faucet with a digital temperature readout or a sink faucet that has an electric eye so it turns on automatically. Even at the home center there are old-looking faucets with metal or porcelain lever or cross handles. A few things to avoid are plastic handles, "two-tone" looks (brass and chrome together), one-handle faucets, permanently shiny brass (it's supposed to tarnish), waterfall spouts, and really contemporary-looking faucets. Fancy faucets with barfing fish spouts are not appropriate for most houses either. Chrome plating is okay as a substitute for nickel. And any kind of showerhead is fine—there are many reproductions being made, or if you really want to have a massaging showerhead, go for it.

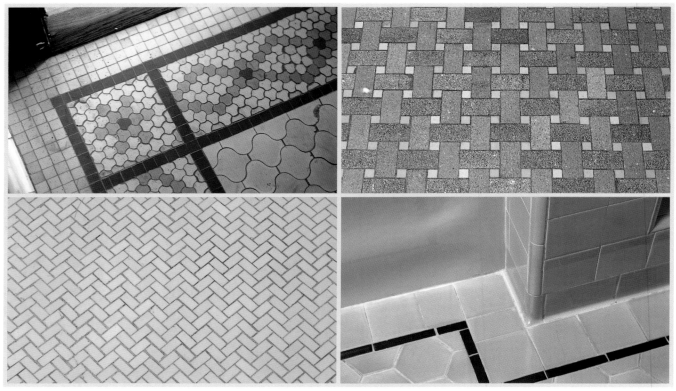

Top left: Unusually shaped mosaic tiles make up a border in a bathroom at the 1907 Dearborn House in Seattle, Washington.
Several different shapes have been used to make a complex floor design for one bathroom in this American foursquare house.
Top right: Mosaic tile in a "woven" pattern decorates the floor of a turquoise-and-lavender bath.
Elaborate colored tile patterns were a hallmark of bathrooms in the 1920s.
Bottom left: Small rectangular mosaics laid in a herringbone pattern make a sanitary floor in the
toilet enclosure of a 1910 home.
Bottom right: Iridescent four-inch hexagonal tiles bordered with black match the square wall tiles in a 1930s bath.

FLOOR PLAY

The best flooring for a bathroom is one that is mostly impervious to water, though not all floors found in historic bathrooms fit that description. By far, the most common type of bathroom flooring is ceramic tile, and the most common kind of ceramic tile is one-inch white hexagons. These were usually unglazed porcelain or vitreous tile, which made them less slippery than glazed tile yet still resistant to dirt and stains. Colored hexagonal tiles were used as accents. Common motifs for accents were single tiles scattered in a diamond pattern (known as a diaper), sets of seven tiles grouped in a "daisy" (the middle tile could be the same color as the others or a different color, like the "eye" of a daisy) or tiles spread in a diaper pattern, arranged in continuous diamonds, or arranged into various border designs. Larger hexagonal tiles (two, three, or four inches) were also used; these sizes tended to have matte glaze, and also came in colors as well as white. The same kind of patterning might be used with the larger sizes, though it was more likely to be limited to diaper patterns rather than borders. Diagonal patterns also made a small bathroom look larger. Other mosaic tiles were also used, such as one-inch squares, two-inch squares, one-inch by two-inch oblongs, or combinations of these. Patterns such as basket weave, herringbone, or even running bond (with offset joints like bricks) were common, as well as the decorative patterns mentioned above. The addition of color opened up whole new opportunities for floors that resembled plaid, woven fabric, etc. Four-inch square tiles with a matte glaze were also used on floors. Even six-inch square tiles made an occasional appearance.

Unlike modern tile, which has eased or pillowed edges, old tile is flat and was usually set with almost nonexistent grout joints (one-sixteenth of an inch or less). Art tiles (mostly in the 1930s) might be set with wider joints, especially if they were "rustic" or hand-made. Grout colors were mostly limited to white, off-white, sand, or gray. And tile was always set on a mortar bed approximately one inch thick (known as a "mud job") until the rather recent invention of cement backer board. A mud job lasts a very long time, with the tile and the mortar functioning as one complete unit. Often, if the house has settled, there will be cracks in the tile itself rather than at the grout joints. Mosaics often came prearranged, with paper on the face to hold them together. The paper had water-soluble glue so it could be removed after the tile was set. Either wooden or tile baseboards were used. Baseboard tile came with either flat or coved bottoms, and flat or bull nose (rounded) tops. Bull-nose tops were used to make a tile baseboard if there was no tile wainscoting above.

Though not that impervious to water, wood was used often for flooring, especially in the nineteenth century and the first two decades of the twentieth. This was almost always tongue-and-groove softwood (fir, pine, or whatever the inexpensive local softwood was at the time) with a clear or painted finish. Hardwood floors were rare. Many wood floors were

Hand-inlaid linoleum squares (by artist Laurie Crogan) add a decorative touch to a simple bathroom in a craftsman bungalow from the teens.

later covered with some other kind of flooring, such as linoleum.

Linoleum was invented by Englishman Frederick Walton in 1863, and was available in America by the 1870s. Composed of ground cork, linseed oil, and fillers on a burlap backing, it has become the generic name for sheet flooring, although it was mostly superseded by vinyl in the 1960s. In the nineteenth century, solid-color "battleship" linoleum and checkerboard-like tile patterns were common, as well as designs printed on the surface of a solid color body. Then Walton discovered ways to integrate the designs into the body during the manufacturing process by mixing the linoleum granules in various ways before they were run through the heated rollers (called calenders) that fused them to the backing, resulting in marble, granite, and jaspé (striated) patterns. Inlaid patterns resembling encaustic tile were produced using a stencil method in which different-colored granules were sprinkled into shaped perforated trays, after which the trays were removed and the sheets run through heated

Terrazzo floors were not terribly common in private residences, owing to their expense, but one was installed in this 1906 Arts and Crafts house. A sink on a fluted pedestal receives abundant natural light from windows on either side of the medicine cabinet, and a stained-glass window in a sailboat design decorates the door. A new toilet has been installed in an angled corner.

rollers, which fused them to the backing. In 1898, Walton invented a process for making straight-line inlaid linoleum that produced crisp geometric designs. In this process, strips of uncured linoleum were cut and pieced like a patchwork quilt before being calendered. Embossed inlaid linoleum, usually found in tile-like patterns, was introduced in 1926. Linoleum could also be inlaid while it was being installed—

usually this took the form of an accent stripe about an inch wide around the edges, but especially in the 1930s and '40s, more elaborate inlays with medallions and other geometric designs were shown, at least in advertisements. From the 1920s to '40s, an explosion of color and pattern took place: Florentine swirls, stylized Art Deco patterns, even Oriental rug designs were produced. Many old linoleum patterns are still available in vinyl, although the really unusual ones are not. A well-cared-for linoleum floor can last a very long time.

Another kind of resilient flooring was introduced in 1910: a bitumen-impregnated felt paper with a printed design on the face. This gave rise to many advertisements urging consumers "for your own protection, learn to tell genuine linoleum: look for the woven burlap back." The designs were similar to linoleum, and this product was especially popular as a rug, although it was also installed wall-to-wall. It didn't wear as well as linoleum because the pattern didn't go all the way through. If old sheet flooring shows black patches in the worn areas, it is probably this material.

Less common but seen occasionally were rubber floor tiles and terrazzo. Rubber floor tiles were introduced in the early 1920s. Available in solid colors or marbleized designs, they were generally laid in a checkerboard pattern. They were more expensive than linoleum, and so were more likely to be found in commercial businesses. Terrazzo floors were introduced in the United States in 1890, but only after the invention of electric grinders for polishing did terrazzo gain acceptance. It was also expensive, limiting it to the homes of the wealthy. It was much more likely to be found in commercial applications, though its use in smaller areas (like shower pans) was a little more widespread.

Stone floors (usually marble) were occasionally found in bathrooms. The marble industry promoted its use, of course, although there was some argument over whether it was "sanitary" or not. Carrera marble (white with bluish-gray veining) was probably the most common, but other colors of marble became more prevalent during the 1920s and later. Other kinds of stone were also used, but infrequently. Most often 12-by-12-inch tiles were used, regardless of the kind of stone. Stone floors were expensive, so it's

unlikely they were found in an average tract bungalow.

Mostly after World War II, other flooring materials such as asphalt tile, vinyl-asbestos tile, and sheet vinyl came into vogue. Often these were applied on top of existing flooring, including ceramic tile. In the 1970s, there was a brief flurry of popularity for bathroom carpeting, which was made of nylon and ostensibly washable, except that a bathroom-sized piece was too big to fit in the average home washing machine. Regular carpeting in the bathroom is generally a bad idea, since there is a likelihood of water damage.

Obsessive Restoration (Flooring)

The biggest enemy of wood floors is water, and bathrooms have a lot of water. Unless kept well sealed, water can cause rot and also staining. (The iron in the nails combines with the tannins in the wood to cause black stains that cannot be sanded or bleached out.) If the wood is still in good shape, it can be refinished. Minor black stains can be ignored; major ones may require replacement of those boards. Try to use old boards from a closet, the attic, or some other hidden space, rather than new boards, as most woods tend to darken with age, and new boards will be lighter. If the floor is too badly stained, it can always be painted. A couple of coats of varnish on top of the paint will help it last longer. For a clear finish, use numerous coats. Technically, varnish should be used (spar varnish is good), as polyurethane hadn't been invented. If a whole new floor is being put in, it is possible to get antique flooring, salvaged from demolished buildings or milled from larger salvaged timbers.

Ceramic tile flooring on a mortar bed will pretty much last forever, as long as the wood underneath remains intact. It may develop cracks, the glaze might wear, and the grout may get stained and dirty, but

Chevrons and diamonds in blue and black are part of an elaborate floor design in a 1929 Mediterranean-style home.

most of this is easily dealt with. Start by cleaning the floor. Use basic household cleaners first—if that doesn't work, go for something stronger, like an acid-based tile and grout cleaner. Use a stiff-bristle toothbrush on the grout. If the grout turns out to be white but is still a little dingy, there are grout whiteners available that, surprisingly, actually work. They usually come in bottles with sponge applicators—it's basically paint that sticks to the grout but can be wiped off the tile once it dries. If there are very large cracks in the tile, it might be good to fill them—use white thin-set mortar with a latex additive. If the tiles are colored, the right color of nail polish can do wonders for touching up, or appliance touch-up paint also works for the basic colors. There's not much to be done about worn patches, except to learn to think of it as patina.

Sometimes the ceramic tile has been covered with some other kind of flooring, such as linoleum, vinyl, or asphalt tile. Usually this was glued directly to the tile and is fairly easy to pull up. (It would be wise to have a sample of it tested for asbestos first—if it tests posi-

tive, removal might best be left to experts.) But after pulling up the other flooring, a lot of glue residue and other gunk may be left. This will generally dissolve in the right solvent—try hot water, mineral spirits, lemon oil, citrus-based strippers, or floor adhesive remover (this is usually methylene chloride—a known carcinogen. Be sure to wear a respirator, as well as hand and eye protection, and dispose of the residue at a local hazardous-materials collection center). Some serious scrubbing may be required to get the residue out of the grout. After it's all cleaned up, it probably wouldn't hurt to seal the floor. Tile stores sell many kinds of sealers, and floor or paste wax also works. And all the joints in a bathroom should be caulked—around the toilet, baseboards, bottom of a pedestal sink, the tub, and the bottom of the vanity or other cabinets—to prevent water penetration.

Moving the fixtures around (particularly the toilet or tub) may require patching the floor, so it's best to avoid this. Otherwise, try to come up with a patch that looks like it was done on purpose as part of the design. (See "Tubs/Showers" for more ideas.)

If the existing floor is beyond saving because of irreparable damage to the tile or rot in the wood underneath, then a new floor can be installed. It's probably best to rip out the existing floor and start over, especially if rot is involved. This will also provide an opportunity to install radiant heating in the floor if desired. Tile floors can be cold—it would be worthwhile to at least install insulation under the floor, especially if it is over an unheated basement or crawl space. A reinforced mortar bed is the traditional way to go, although plywood and cement backer board will also work.

There are some things to consider when using new tiles. Most old tiles were flat rather than having eased edges as modern tiles do (although it is still possible to get flat tiles). Most modern tiles also have spacing "lugs" on the sides, which give a wider grout joint (usually about one-eighth inch, as opposed to one-sixteenth for old tiles). The spacing lugs will have to be cut off for smaller joints. An exception to this is art tiles from the 1920s or '30s, which were meant to have wider joints, up to one-quarter inch. Also, mosaic tiles now come on sheets with one-eighth-inch joints—if the joints are to be smaller, the sheets will have to be cut apart. It is still possible to buy mosaics in individual pieces. Some companies will also assemble custom borders or sheets based on your designs. You can also assemble your own designs at home. It's best to lay the whole thing out dry first and label it very carefully. Floor tiles should be unglazed or matte glazed—shiny glazes are too slippery for floors. Unglazed tiles should be sealed, especially if they are not vitreous or porcelain. It is also possible to tile over an existing floor, assuming the substrate is in good condition. (Be sure to use latex admixture in the thin-set.) This will make the floor higher, though, and may require adjustments at plumbing fixtures or doorways. Speaking of doorways, many bathrooms featured a marble threshold as a transition to another floor surface.

Linoleum in a bathroom needs to be kept well sealed; otherwise it can rot, since it is not impervious to water. Often it was varnished for this purpose, or else wax was used. The same is true of bitumen-impregnated asphalt floors. If the floors are still in good condition, by all means keep them. Otherwise, new linoleum is available. Sheet linoleum is generally better than linoleum tiles for bathrooms—water penetration between the tiles can be a problem. Early on, linoleum was laid flat up to a wooden baseboard,

Four-inch hexagonal tiles with a crystalline orchid-and-yellow glaze feature a yellow-and-black border. The conservative architecture of the brick-fronted 1931 Tudor gives no clue as to the wildly colored bath waiting inside.

sometimes with a shoe molding. (These joints should be caulked.) Later in the 1920s, it was coved—that is, curved up the wall a couple of inches, making it easier to clean. New linoleum can still be varnished, or either wax or acrylic sealers can be used. Bathrooms in the 1930s and '40s often had elaborate linoleum inlay, which it is still possible for a skilled installer to replicate. Make sure you find someone who has experience with linoleum—it tends to stretch and shrink and is not the same as laying vinyl.

Stone or marble floors are subject to the same problems as tile. Marble in particular is quite porous and stains easily. Special cleaners are made for marble and stone. Avoid cleaners containing acid. Once the stone is cleaned, it should be sealed. If it needs to be replaced, see hints under "Tile." Terrazzo floors or shower pans should be repaired by professionals.

Compromise Solution

There's not much need to compromise on wood floors, as long as they're wood. Laminate floors are not really appropriate. For one thing, most of them have particleboard cores that are not water-resistant. Second, if you wouldn't put wood-grain laminate on a countertop, why would you put it on the floor?

Eased-edge ceramic tiles will be fine for the floor, and wider grout joints won't be that noticeable either. Avoid 12-by-12-inch tiles (unless they're stone), as they look too modern. Stick to mosaics and 4-by-4-inch (or smaller) sizes. As mentioned above, custom borders can be ordered or you can make up your own. If it's a new installation, try to blend it with the existing wall tile (if any)—don't just get white if everything else is yellow and green. Either a mortar bed or cement backer board can be used as a substrate for the tile—again, a new installation is a chance to install radiant heating in the floor.

Linoleum is better than vinyl, as vinyl tends to be much too shiny. A few vinyls have sort of a matte finish, and these are a little more acceptable. Either way, they should be installed either flat to the baseboard or coved. Don't use that dreadful glue-on vinyl baseboard. Vinyl tile has the same drawback as linoleum tile—a tendency for water to penetrate into the seams between the tiles.

Stone for floors was mostly limited to marble. This was not the currently trendy tumbled marble or mosaics that will brand a bathroom as belonging to the turn of the twenty-first century, much as one might like to think it makes it look like ancient Rome.

Carpeting, though lovely on the feet, is generally a bad idea in bathrooms. Area rugs are perfectly acceptable, though this is not where you want to use the priceless Orientals.

An Eastlake washstand with a marble top has been converted to a plumbed vanity with an unusual faucet. Since this is a new bathroom in a 1907 Arts and Crafts house, the owners went with an eclectic look using crackle glazed subway tile, a claw-foot tub, and an inset of English Arts and Crafts tiles (shown on page 121).

VANITY FLAIR (CABINETS)

In the nineteenth century, bathrooms were furnished very much like other rooms in the house, and the fixtures were encased in cabinetry. This was especially true of lavatories, which had started as washstands before they were permanently plumbed. Adding a little storage for the various bathroom accoutrements made sense. With the rise of the "sanitary" bathroom, most cabinetry was done away with, as it was believed to harbor germs. Exceptions to this customarily included built-in medicine cabinets or linen closets. Wooden medicine cabinets were usually recessed into the wall between the studs, and a linen closet often took up the excess space at one end of the tub. Sometimes this took the form of a "linen press," a wider closet with horizontal doors that opened on spring-loaded hinges. The medicine cabinet was normally located over the sink, but not always. Sometimes the lower part of the cabinet was an open shelf or had a horizontal door that opened to become

Black-and-pink marble tops a large vanity in the master bath of a 1929 Mediterranean.
It is made to resemble a piece of furniture and sits on an interesting patterned-tile floor.

Nickel-plated classically styled legs dress up a marble lavatory, complemented by a corner cabinet with an angled mirror, in the 1901 Stimson-Green Mansion. Leaf-patterned wall sconces flank the mirror, and a pink border provides a touch of color in the tile wainscot.

a shelf. Usually the upper door was mirrored. The doors were frame-and-panel, with square stiles and rails around a flat panel or mirror. Generally these were inset flush with the face frame, although in the 1920s and beyond, overlay-style frame-and-panel doors were also used. Metal medicine cabinets began to be used in the 1930s. Although most medicine cabinets had only one door, multiple-door models that took up more than one stud bay were also pretty com-

mon. Cabinets that sat on the floor lacked the toe kicks that modern cabinets sport, at least until the 1920s, when toe kicks that were lower and shallower than today's first made an appearance. Bathroom counters were and continue to be lower than kitchen cabinets (about twenty-nine inches without tops, as opposed to thirty-four inches for kitchen cabinets), possibly so children would find it easier to reach the sink.

Many houses had cabinets scattered around the bathroom: cabinets on either side of a pedestal sink, a cabinet under the window, a tall storage cabinet in a corner, corner cabinets, laundry hampers, laundry chutes, almost anything you can think of. Some even had dressing tables or vanities (a sink set into a cabinet). A few had stools or chairs that folded out of the wall for seating. On the other hand, some houses had nothing more than a medicine cabinet for bathroom storage.

Bathroom cabinets would have been made of the local inexpensive softwood of the time (vertical-grain Douglas fir, heart pine, and so forth). Hardwoods were generally not used, except in the Victorian period. In the twentieth century, the majority of these cabinets would have been painted, the sanitarians having triumphed in the bathroom even more than in the kitchen. White, off-white, cream, beige, pale yellow, or gray were common colors. With the advent of wildly colored tile, paint colors got a little wild as well.

Painted sage green, a marble-topped hutch furnishes ample storage for a new bathroom in a 1908 plan-book bungalow by Henry L. Wilson. Frosted glass in the upper doors disguises the contents.

Obsessive Restoration (Cabinets)

Although plywood had been invented, cabinet sides, door panels, and drawer bottoms were made of edge-glued boards. Shop-built cabinets had backs of 1-by-4-inch tongue-and-groove beaded paneling. Some cabinets were built in place and had the plaster wall as a back. Although any home magazine will tell you that dovetail joints are the mark of a well-crafted drawer, all the original drawers I have seen have half-lap or butt joints held together with glue and nails. The drawer face forms the fourth side of the drawer box, unlike in modern construction where the face is applied to an already completed box.

Sometimes the drawer has a U-shaped wooden runner on the bottom that slides along a piece of wood inside the cabinet; otherwise, the sides of the drawer slide along a frame inside the cabinet. Doorframes and face frames were usually constructed using blind mortise-and-tenon joinery, but other kinds of joinery will also work. If the new doors are to be as thick as the old doors, construct them using 5/4 stock (a one by four isn't as thick as it used to be). The glass or mirror in glass doors is held in place by small square or quarter-round moldings attached with brads. The truly obsessive will want to use old wavy glass.

Shelves could be either fixed or adjustable. Fixed shelves either sat on cleats or were glued into a groove cut into the side of the cabinet. Adjustable shelves sat on cleats that fit into slots cut out of half-inch by one-inch strips of wood nailed to the sides of the cabinet. The ends of the shelves were notched to fit over the strips. Metal shelf pins that fit into drilled holes were also used. Some medicine cabinets had glass shelves—these were held up by metal pins or metal clips that slipped into narrow slots cut in the cabinet sides. Glass shelves were more common in metal medicine cabinets.

Sometimes the original cabinets got a facelift in the 1950s or '60s and acquired new slab doors. These can be replaced with proper frame-and-panel doors; however, overlay rather than inset doors will fit better in this case, as the old openings will not be square, and inset doors have fairly close tolerances.

As mentioned above, a majority of bathroom cabinets would have been painted, with only a few exceptions. Oil-based paint would have been used at the time. The few clear-finished cabinets would have had shellac or varnish. Shellac doesn't hold up very well to water or alcohol, but old shellac has a dipped-in-honey quality that is quite lovely. A topcoat of varnish over the shellac will preserve the look while adding a bit more protection.

A recessed metal medicine cabinet with a Tudor-arch mirror is surrounded by a ceramic hook, toothbrush holder, soap dish, and shelf supports for a glass shelf. The mirror is dramatically framed by imported Italian border tile, which was expensive even at the time this 1932 house was built.

Compromise Solution

It is perfectly legitimate to add storage to a bathroom that may only have a medicine cabinet. Recessing cabinets between the studs works well, as it doesn't take up space in the room and many bathroom products will fit in a shallow space. A shallow cabinet over the toilet tank is useful. Perhaps replacing a wall-hung or pedestal sink with a vanity will provide more storage. Freestanding cabinets can also be used, or other wall-hung or corner cabinets as space allows.

Plywood will make perfectly acceptable sides, backs, drawer bottoms, and door panels. Avoid MDF (medium-density fiberboard) and particleboard—they do not hold up well in a wet environment. Have cabinets with a toe kick if you like. Plywood paneling that resembles bead board is available for visible cabinet backs. There is no substitute for frame-and-panel doors, but biscuit or other types of joinery would work as well as mortise-and-tenon. Doors made with 1-by-4 stock will not be as thick as old doors, but this will not be very noticeable. Glass can be mounted using silicone adhesive rather than molding. Drawer boxes can be made in the modern manner and run on metal glides. Center-mount glides that don't show when the drawer is open are another option. Modern shelf mounting systems—either pins that fit into drilled holes or clips that fit into metal tracks—will work. The drilled-hole method is less visually obtrusive in a glass door cabinet. Self-adhesive shelf covering (first manufactured in 1949) is acceptable.

Only Victorian bathrooms had furniture. Try to avoid the "Arts and Crafts Revival" look: fumed-oak vanity with hammered-copper hardware, granite top, art-glass light fixtures, etc., unless you are building a brand-new house.

Counter Act (Countertops)

The most common countertop in bathrooms was probably tile. Starting with the washstands of the Victorian period, tile was used both for countertops and backsplashes. Later, its identification with cleanliness and sanitation made it the most common choice as vanity cabinets began to appear, and even for the tops of other cabinets. As with floors, one-inch white hexagons, sometimes with a pattern in contrasting colors, were the most common. Other kinds of small mosaics, larger glazed hexagons, or 3-by-3 or 4-by-4-inch tiles, as well as 3-by-5 or 3-by-6-inch oblong "subway" tiles were also popular. Either white or wildly colored tiles were used, depending on the year of the bathroom and the style of the house. Edge tiles were generally box-edge or ogee (shaped like modern V-cap edging but with a more pronounced curve). Quarter-round tiles were used as edging and also around tile-in sinks. (A round tile-in sink requires the quarter-round to be cut up into one-inch pieces to outline the sink.)

Tile was laid on a wire-reinforced mortar bed approximately one inch thick. Grout joints were minimal, 1/16 inch or less. Mosaics came in sheets with a paper backing on the face. After the tile was set, the backing was sponged with water till the glue dissolved and the paper could be peeled off. Sometimes three- and four-inch-square tiles were laid on the diagonal with a square border around the edge. Colored accent tiles were often set into the countertop or the backsplash.

The second most common countertop material was marble, especially in the Victorian period, but even into the 1930s. A ceramic bowl set under a marble slab, held up by legs or a cabinet, is common in all periods. Occasionally some other sort of stone was used, but marble was the most common.

Wood was also used, especially on cabinets that didn't have a sink in them, although it was also found as a countertop around sinks. Usually painted, it was sometimes also given a clear finish. Occasionally wood got covered with linoleum at a later date.

Much more rarely, countertops of Monel metal (a nickel alloy) or even structural glass (Vitrolite) were employed. This was much more likely in the 1930s and beyond.

Obsessive Restoration (Countertops)

An existing tile countertop should be kept if possible. Often cleaning, regrouting, or some minor repair is all that's needed. (There are companies who offer this service, or you can do it yourself.) If the dirt doesn't respond to regular cleaners, try an acid-based tile-and-grout cleaner. Broken or gouged tiles can be repaired with thin-set mortar and then touched up with paint or nail polish. (Conveniently, nail polish now comes in just about any color you can imagine.) Broken edge tiles can be a problem—look in the basement, garage, attic, or crawl space to see if possibly a few extras were saved from the installation.

Tile was laid on a mortar bed consisting of the following layers: rough wood planks covered with a layer of building felt (tar paper), then wire-mesh reinforcing (chicken wire) held by bent-over nails, followed by a layer of mortar about an inch thick, over which the tile was laid. Tiles were spaced very closely so grout joints were minimal. Box-cap edging is difficult to find, but box edging is still available from some manufacturers. There are a couple of ways to use it: cut off one leg of the U and run it vertically, or use it horizontally on top of the counter, with one leg hanging off the edge and sitting on either a strip of wood or a row of 3-by-6-inch-surface bull-nose edging tiles. The other problem with modern box-edge is the dearth of accompanying trim pieces such as outside corners and end pieces, which results in corners having to be mitered. Also available was ogee edging (S-shaped), similar to modern V-cap edging but with a more rounded profile. Modern V-cap came into production after World War II.

Old tile is sharp-edged, unlike modern tile, which has eased edges. (Some flat tile is still made.) Modern tile also tends to come with spacing lugs, which results in wider grout joints; these can be cut off with a wet saw for closer spacing. Handmade or art tile, on the other hand, requires wider grout joints. One-inch hexagonal tile is still widely sold—the unglazed is better in vitreous or porcelain, the soft-body hexagonal tile will need to be sealed. Old-style mosaics (usually a combination of 1- and 2-inch squares with 1-by-2-inch oblongs) are becoming more readily available. Four-by-four-inch tiles are quite common, though 3-by-3-inch tiles are somewhat harder to procure. Salvaged tiles are a possibility, especially for a small area, since it is not always possible to find sufficient quantities for a large area. Many contemporary tile companies and craftspeople are making hand-

A basin set in a Carrera-marble slab with an integral shell-shaped soap dish features a high marble backsplash and Fuller ball faucets.

made tile—use this only if it is appropriate to the period and style of your house (for example, built late 1920s to '30s).

Marble countertops share similar problems with tile. Often they are stained or cracked. Special cleaners and poultices are made for stone and marble. Once cleaned, they should be sealed with an impregnating sealer to protect them.

Salvage dealers frequently have marble sink tops and countertops in quantity. Sink tops already have holes for basins and faucets. These have more patina than a new top, although a new top is certainly an option. A new top should be a slab, though: marble tiles were generally used only on floors.

Wooden countertops were often made of one piece of wood (1 or 2 inches thick by up to 24 inches wide). At the present time, it is difficult, though not impossible, to get a piece of wood this size. In the high humidity environment of a bathroom, a plank that wide is likely to cup or crack; so smaller edge-glued boards were used instead. Sometimes an edge detailing or a small piece of molding finished off the edge. If clear-finished, these should have numerous coats of shellac or varnish. If painted, oil-based paint in the usual bathroom colors was traditionally used.

Linoleum was often added to wooden countertops at a later date, although in the 1930s and '40s linoleum countertops were a style unto themselves. Linoleum countertops should have a metal or wooden edge, and need to be either varnished or periodically given a coat of paste wax or floor wax. Replacement linoleum is also a possibility if the existing linoleum is too far gone.

Monel metal should not have been exposed to too much hard wear in a bathroom. It should be cleaned using a neutral pH soap and warm water. To remove paint, use paint remover (be sure to wear a respirator and other protective gear). Stains may respond to a slurry of oxalic acid and powdered pumice applied with a brush. Plastic or nylon pads can also be used. Once it is clean, it can be lacquered for protection.

Structural glass is no longer produced in America, although it is produced in limited sizes and colors in Czechoslovakia and Japan and imported to the U.S. Occasionally pieces can be found at glass dealers or salvage yards. If the existing structural glass is in good shape, it may only require cleaning. Cracks can be filled with caulking tinted to match the glass. Chips and holes can be repaired by filling with polyester resin adhesive tinted to match the glass. The surface can then be polished with fine sandpaper and buffed with polish. Another method is to fill the hole with glazing compound and then paint the area with computer-matched paint color. Other substitutes for structural glass include back-painted flat glass, acrylic sheets, and laminated glass, but none of these perfectly replicates the qualities of the historic material.

Compromise Solution

Much period-looking tile is still sold in all price ranges. Modern white glazes tend to be much whiter than their period counterparts, so look for antique white, cream, or almond. In colored tiles, similar colors to those used in the 1920s and '30s are also obtainable. Mosaic tiles (1- and 2-inch hexagonal, 1-and 2-inch squares) usually come in sheets spaced for 1/8-inch grout joints. If you want smaller joints, the sheets have to be cut up and the tiles placed individually. Modern V-cap is fine for edging. Try to avoid tiles larger than 4 1/4 by 4 1/4—larger tiles usually look too modern, although some handmade or art tiles are larger. Rope inlays and edging that resembles elaborate crown molding are usually not appropriate unless there is precedent for it elsewhere in the house.

Setting the tile on cement backer board with thin-set mortar is an acceptable method. Don't go crazy with colored grout: white, off-white, sand, beige, and gray were pretty much the period colors, although art tile might have had dark gray or brown.

Try to stick with salvaged or simple marble slabs (again, unless there's some precedent in another bathroom). Occasionally other kinds of stone were used, but marble was the most common. Usually a honed rather than polished finish is best. And forget the currently trendy tumbled marble—it's just so twenty-first century. Solid surfacing should not be used either—it looks too fake. Besides, if you can afford solid surfacing, you can afford marble instead—it's about the same price. If you are on a very small budget, some of the vaguely stone-like laminates don't look too bad, especially with a wooden edge treatment, but try to avoid the prefabricated, post-formed laminate counters that are sold at home centers. Concrete counters are also currently trendy—don't even think about it. Terrazzo is more acceptable.

A plywood counter with a wood strip or molding on the front edge is a reasonable substitute for solid wood. If a clear finish is used, especially around a sink, put on lots of coats. Polyurethane is okay, although the water-based kind tends to get cloudy-looking if too many coats build up. If the wood is to be painted, either oil-based (alkyd) or latex paint will work.

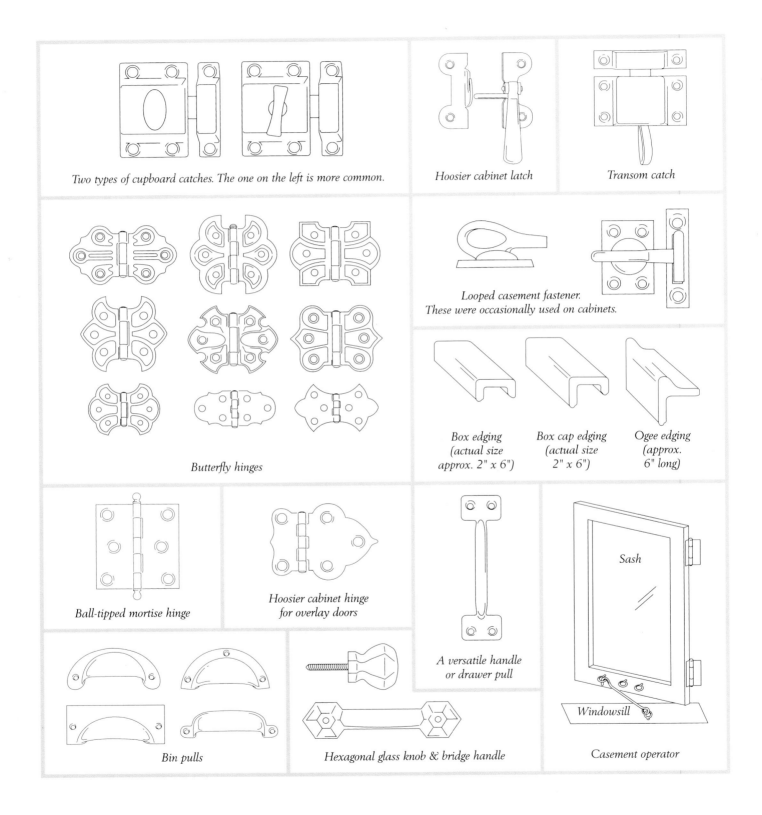

Two types of cupboard catches. The one on the left is more common.

Hoosier cabinet latch

Transom catch

Butterfly hinges

*Looped casement fastener.
These were occasionally used on cabinets.*

*Box edging
(actual size
approx. 2" x 6")*

*Box cap edging
(actual size
2" x 6")*

*Ogee edging
(approx.
6" long)*

Ball-tipped mortise hinge

*Hoosier cabinet hinge
for overlay doors*

*A versatile handle
or drawer pull*

Sash

Windowsill

Bin pulls

Hexagonal glass knob & bridge handle

Casement operator

Knob Scene (Hardware)

Three-tiered towel bars allow more towels to be hung in a smaller space, as this model at the Stimson-Green Mansion illustrates.

A combination towel rack and bar provides storage for extra towels in a bath at the Stimson-Green Mansion in Seattle.

Period hardware is remarkably standardized. There are only about twelve different kinds of hinges, pulls, and knobs, with a few style variations in each category. Window hardware styles were equally limited. Most cabinet doors were hinged with either 2 1/2- inch ball-tipped mortise hinges (a mortise is a shallow cutout the same depth as the thickness of the hinge leaf) or surface-mounted butterfly hinges. Overlay doors used special surface-mounted offset hinges. Butterfly hinges came in a few basic shapes. Passage doors used three-inch mortise hinges, usually ball-tipped, though fancier tips were available, and had either brass, nickel-plated, or glass doorknobs on mortised (set into the door stile) locks.

The most common cabinet door hardware in bathrooms is probably the hexagonal glass knob, either clear or in various colors, followed by the spring-loaded cupboard turn. Overlay doors closed with special offset latches, like those used on Hoosier cabinets. Metal knobs (brass, nickel, or chrome) made an occasional appearance, and a few houses even featured wrought-iron hardware.

Drawers used hexagonal glass knobs, glass "bridge" handles (two hexagonal knobs connected with a glass bridge), bin pulls, metal drawer pulls, or metal knobs. Metal hardware was either nickel- (more common) or brass-plated (till chrome plating began to appear in the late 1920s and '30s). Most of the hardware was not solid brass but plating over base metal, and most

Glass rods with metal supports were a common kind of towel bar, as shown here in the 1899 Dunsmuir House in Oakland, California.

common, as well as metal ends with glass bars. All-metal, porcelain-and-metal, all-wood, or even all-ceramic towel bars were found. Both single and double rods were used, in various lengths. Towel racks (often mounted over the toilet) were usually metal, and might have bars for hanging as well as open shelving for folded towels.

Toilet paper holders fall into two categories: recessed and not recessed. Special wall-mounted boxes for single-sheet paper were available in metal, wood, and ceramic (not very common in America, where roll paper was more popular, but there are a few). Wall-hung holders, often with the familiar spring-loaded roller (made of wood back then,

pieces were stamped rather than cast.

Double-hung windows used the still-ubiquitous sash locks and lifts; casement windows used hardware similar to modern hardware, although many houses had a looped-style turn that is difficult to find now. Casement operators often consisted of a hook-and-eye system, where the hook was eight to twelve inches long and screwed into the sill, and eyes located in various places on the sash controlled how far the window opened. More formal casement operators were also used. Operable transom windows used special catches similar to cupboard catches.

Other hardware specific to bathrooms includes towel bars; toilet-paper holders; toothbrush, glass, and soap holders; hooks; towel racks; shelf brackets; shower rods; etc. Towel bars could be made of metal, ceramic, glass, wood, or combinations of these materials. Ceramic end pieces with a wooden or glass bar were

later of metal or plastic) came in metal, wood, and ceramic. Even freestanding holders that sat on the floor next to the toilet were sold. Recessed holders of ceramic or metal were very common, and still are. Glass shelves on metal or ceramic brackets were quite widespread, especially with wall-hung or pedestal sinks, which don't provide much counter space. Hooks for robes or towels or for holding the razor strop (for those still using straight razors) were usually metal or ceramic. Shower rods were usually metal, either brass- or nickel-plated, and chrome-plated after the 1920s. These were permanently attached, unlike the spring-loaded rods available today. The end pieces were generally round, although some stylized end pieces (triangles, etc.) appeared during the ArtDeco period. Soap dishes, toothbrush holders, water glass holders, jewel cups for women's jewelry, and even match holders and cigar rests for men were all built into or attached to the wall. These items were generally attached one of two ways: ceramic items were mortared directly onto the wall as part of the tile pattern, or else a channel in the back of the piece slid over a metal bracket that was attached to the wall so the pieces could be removed for cleaning. This method was also used for metal hardware.

Obsessive Restoration (Hardware)

You might find that existing hardware has been covered with paint. (There is a special ring of Hell reserved for people who paint over sash locks!) Once you get the hardware off, soak it in a strong mixture of trisodium phosphate and hot water (about one tablespoon per cup of water) to remove the paint. Paint stripper will also work. Numerous layers may require more soaking. Paint doesn't stick to ceramic very well, so ceramic pieces are particularly easy to strip.

The hardware may or may not be in good shape once the paint is off—it might be easier to buy new hardware, since most of the old styles are still being made. Hardware stores still carry cupboard turns, various styles of butterfly hinges, brass drawer pulls, and porcelain knobs, as well as sash locks and casement hardware (including operators). Ball-tipped mortise hinges, Hoosier-type hinges and latches, hexagonal glass knobs, glass bridge handles and bin pulls, and any nickel-plated pieces are available through catalogs and specialty retailers, as are mortise locks and all kinds of doorknobs. Casement latches with a loop-style turn, which were extremely common in the period, are quite difficult to find now. Salvage yards are the best source for these. Metal hardware can also be replated. This is best if the existing hardware is unusual and not easy to replicate.

Often existing ceramic pieces will be broken—anything that sticks out from the wall is particularly

Metal cup holders, toilet-paper holders, sponge holders, and wall-mounted mirrors are shown here at the Vintage Plumbing showroom in Northridge, California.

Ceramic towel bar supports, soap dish, toothbrush rack, and cup holder complement the orchid pedestal sink in this iridescent-tile bath.

stripped of its chrome to get to the nickel underneath, but the nickel isn't that thick and will not hold up to wear very well.

One final obsessive note: Use only slotted screws! Although Phillips screws had been invented, they were not used residentially till much later. You may have to buy extra slotted screws to replace the Phillips screws that come with new hardware.

Compromise Solution

Hardware is like jewelry for the bathroom. The interplay of doors, drawers, hinges, and knobs is an important part of the design. Hinges were meant to be visible, and there were no hidden self-adjusting European hinges during the period. Though cabinet-makers like the European hinges because they are easier to install, cabinets without visible hinges just don't look right. Surface-mounted hinges are slightly easier to work with than mortise hinges (which may placate the cabinetmaker). Since appropriate period hardware is available, there is really no need to compromise on that. And try not to get carried away with cast-brass fish or seashells for knobs.

Some modern styles of towel bars and such should be avoided, such as those made of plastic, particularly the kind where the bar itself curves back toward the wall on the ends. A lot of modern towel bars may have ceramic ends and plastic bars—not much to be done about that. All-metal may be a better choice. Avoid very contemporary-looking pieces—there are plenty of retro-looking accessories and hardware that will work just fine. As mentioned above, permanently installed shower rods are still sold, but a spring-loaded rod is okay as well.

Red ceramic hooks are set into the wall tile in an amazing red-and-black bathroom from 1932, providing a handy place to hang a robe or a towel.

prone to this. If you have the pieces, it can be glued back together and possibly touched up with nail polish. If it's missing, it will be a little more problematic. Salvage yards do carry various ceramic accessories, but finding one that matches, especially if you have colored tile, can take quite a hunt. It might be better to either live with it or get a metal replacement.

It is still possible to buy a permanently installed metal shower rod—this may involve drilling holes in the tile, for which special drill bits are available. Usually these rods are chrome or brass—nickel will be harder to come by. It is possible to have a chrome rod

Light streams through leaded-glass casement windows set into Douglas-fir frames, illuminating a restored bathroom with bead-board wainscoting, a stenciled cabinet, and a reproduction beaded pillbox toilet. This room had been badly remodeled by a previous owner of the 1918 bungalow.

MULLION IT OVER (WINDOWS AND DOORS)

Most bathrooms had at least one window, sometimes more, although there were a few land-locked bathrooms that had none. Windows were generally double-hung or casement, although occasionally other styles such as hopper, awning, or sliding windows put in an appearance.

Wood was the most common material for windows, although some house styles (Tudor, Moderne) had metal windows. A few houses, especially from the 1930s and beyond, had glass block windows. The window glass could be clear or obscure (translucent), and occasionally art glass was used, although this was much more common in the Victorian period than in the twentieth century. Etched glass was also used.

English stained-glass windows (one fixed, flanked by two casements) were picked up at a salvage yard and installed to lend privacy to the bead-board-lined tub room of a 1909 Arts and Crafts–style home. The tub is original to the house, although it has been moved. Bead board was often used because it was cheaper than plaster, though this is no longer the case.

Sometimes only the bottom sash of a double-hung window had obscure glass, while the top sash was clear. The sash was either plain (one-light) or matched the muntin (muntins are the horizontal bars that divide the glass, while mullions are the vertical bars) pattern of the other windows in the house. A bathroom window tended to be smaller and set higher in the wall than a window in an adjoining bedroom would have been. Skylights were sometimes used if no outside wall was available for a window, and of course, many apartment bathrooms have windows that open onto light wells in the center of the building. Sometimes the window was over the tub, a style particularly prevalent in the 1940s. In combination with a shower, this almost invariably leads to rot.

Bathroom doors were either plain wood that

In-swinging casement windows ventilate a large, approximately 9-by-15-foot, bath in a 1915 bungalow. Unfortunately, two of the original porcelain cross handles on the tub have been replaced with modern ones, but the rest of the bathroom is remarkably intact, and except for its large size, is very typical of bungalow bathrooms in the first two decades of the twentieth century.

matched the other doors in the house, or sometimes had obscure glass to allow light to filter into the hallway from the bathroom, and vice versa. One light at the top was common, as well as eight- or ten-light French doors. Art glass was sometimes used, but not commonly. Transoms (a window, usually operable, set over a door) were fairly common in the nineteenth century, less common in the twentieth. Bathroom doors usually had locks for privacy. As a rule, the inside hardware would be nickel-plated to match the other bath hardware, while on the hallway side it would be brass (or match the other hardware in the house). Some bathrooms could have as many as three doors: two from adjoining bedrooms and one from the hall.

A beautiful art-glass door leads into the hall bath of the 1908 Gamble House. The architects, Charles and Henry Greene, were unusual in that they lavished design attention even on utilitarian spaces such as bathrooms, kitchens, and basements. Still, except for the door and the cloud-lift patterns of the window muntins, this bathroom is like any other of the same period.

Obsessive Restoration (Windows and Doors)

Wooden windows, especially double-hung windows, often suffer from broken sash cords or from being painted shut, but are easily repaired. Rotted sashes can also be replaced. A window over a tub should be kept obsessively caulked and sealed. Tempered glass may be required for some windows. Most obscure glass had a sort of "pebbled" effect—this kind of glass is still available. (The smooth side should go on the outside.) Metal windows, especially steel, are harder to repair, but there are companies that repair steel windows. If the entire window needs to be replaced, it will probably have to meet current code, which in most places means at least double glazing. Double-glazed windows look different in subtle ways from old windows, so keep that in mind. Skylights for land-locked bathrooms should be wire glass or "roof window" types, not plastic bubbles. Glass block may suffer from cracks or chips— these usually do not affect the structure. Broken blocks are difficult to replace, both because the installation is essentially masonry, possibly requiring the whole thing to be taken apart, and because it is difficult to match old glass-block patterns, although glass block is still being manufactured. As always, a salvage yard is the best bet for replacements. Otherwise, it may be necessary to

A lavender glass doorknob matches the tile in the main bath of a 1929 Spanish Revival home.

A glass-block window was added to this powder room during the 1930s Deco remodel, which must look a little strange on the outside of the 1902 Colonial Revival residence. (Photo © Stephen J. Shaluta)

replace the entire window with new glass block.

Doors don't usually require too much restoration, unless they are coming apart or have been replaced with modern doors, in which case it's time for a trip to the salvage yard, or to have a new door built. Often the hardware will need to be stripped of paint, or possibly a replacement knob may be needed. It's even possible, by removing the mortise lock and taking it to a locksmith, to have a new key made to replace a missing one.

Compromise Solution

Period bathrooms were not meant to have a wall of windows. It is possible to add one or two more without compromising the historic integrity too much—they should match the existing window(s) as closely as possible. Try to match the muntin pattern (or lack thereof) to the other windows in the house. And it goes without saying that aluminum sliders should be replaced with something more appropriate.

Avoid plastic bubble skylights by using the flat "roof window" type. Glass block now also comes in acrylic: lighter in weight and unbreakable, this can be a good choice for a bathroom in which glass block would be appropriate (after 1930).

Inappropriate "slab" doors should be replaced with frame-and-panel doors. Use wooden doors, not fiberglass with stamped "wood grain." Period-style door hardware is widely obtainable.

High wainscoting of clear-finished bead board sits on top of a wide three-part baseboard under a coved ceiling. A salvaged sink with separate hot and cold taps, an original wooden medicine cabinet set off by porcelain sconces, and a mosaic-tile floor add to the period look for a restored bathroom in a 1918 bungalow.

Flat Douglas-fir moldings frame a mirror, corner medicine cabinet, and stained-glass window in this new powder room, as well as provide mounting for brass-and-glass towel bars. A cast-iron rolled-rim corner sink sports separate cross-handled hot and cold taps.

Lavender, blue, yellow, and green tile surrounds a cornflower-blue tub in an arched niche, demonstrating the "anything goes" theory of color as applied to bathrooms in the 1920s and 1930s. The distortion caused by the wide-angled camera lens makes this tub appear shorter and deeper—it is actually a typical five-foot bathtub.

Lath of the Mohicans (Walls and Ceilings)

Walls and ceilings were mostly made of smooth-finished plaster over wood lath (later metal lath), then painted with enamel. Typically bathroom ceilings were the same height as the rest of the house—eight to ten feet (somewhat higher in the nineteenth century). Commonly, the walls and ceiling met at right angles, although coved ceilings were sometimes seen. As a rule the entire wall and ceiling was plastered, but often the ceiling and upper wall were plastered while the lower wall consisted of wooden wainscoting, either bead board, board-and-batten, or ceramic tile. To save money, the plaster could be scored to look like tile and was sometimes finished with a glaze over the paint to make it appear more tile-like. For those to whom money was no object, on the other hand, a ceramic tile wainscoting could extend all the way to the ceiling (though four feet high was the norm). Some authorities at the time felt that wooden wainscoting was not sanitary, but that didn't stop many builders from installing it anyway.

There was a tendency for wood trim to be simpler in the bathroom than in the rest of the

Top: Aquatic-themed decorative tile insets such as this water lily were common in bathrooms. On the other hand, this color of purple tile is not that common, and may contain radioactive ingredients in the glaze, according to the company that tried to duplicate this color for the homeowner.
Middle: This must be one of the hundred thousand goldfish, mentioned by House and Garden *magazine, installed over the tub in a 1927 Spanish Revival house.*
Bottom: A shell and ribbon border tile tops the subway-tile wainscot in a way that is stylistically appropriate to the Colonial Revival architecture of the 1899 Dunsmuir House.

house, though not always. Door and window trim customarily ran to four or five inches wide, with five- to seven-inch baseboards. It could be either flat or detailed in some way. Sometimes a 1-by-4-inch board ran around the room for mounting towel bars. Trim was usually painted.

Bathroom walls and ceilings were usually painted with enamel for ease of cleaning, even if wainscoting, trim, or cabinets were varnished. Colors ran to the "sanitary": off-white, cream, ivory, or beige. More color was added in the 1920s, but still tended toward pastels such as green, gray, pink, blue, or yellow. Things got a little wilder in the 1930s and after.

Tile wainscoting, tub surrounds, etc., tended to be white until the 1920s, although more colored and decorative tile was seen in the nineteenth century. Hints of color started to sneak in during the teens, usually as small borders or liners on a white background. But in the 1920s, after decades of sanitary white bathrooms, there was a huge explosion of colored tile, and later in the decade, colored fixtures. It was literally "anything goes": lavender and green, pink and green, any color with black, all black, yellow and purple, iridescent turquoise, burgundy, jade; solid colors, mottled patterns, crystalline patterns—and that's just the individual tiles. They were combined into checkerboards, triangles, murals, plaids, stripes, and medallions. Borders and liners ranging from flowers, waves, Art Deco patterns, geometric abstracts, and checkerboards went up on bathroom walls everywhere. Arched and stepped niches were tiled in two, three, four, or more colors. In the 1930s, art tile began to be used: landscape tiles, rustic tiles, lion's heads. It was an amazing display of exuberance that hasn't been seen since. Even the most conservative of houses (say a Stockbroker Tudor) might be hiding a bathroom of unbelievable whimsy and charm. Spanish-style houses were particularly susceptible, but many

A recently restored hand-painted mural decorates the wall above the subway-tile wainscoting at the 1911 Lanterman House.

Stenciling decorates the walls of a bath in a late-nineteenth-century Queen Anne cottage. Dark-stained bead-board wainscoting, a marble-topped lavatory with Fuller ball faucets, and a collection of vintage bath supplies evoke the late-Victorian era of the house.

is skim-coat plaster over blueboard (special water-resistant drywall).

Here are some 1906 directions for faux tile: "When nearly dry, (plaster) should be lightly marked off with a mason's jointing tool into squares, and later, if desired, painted with four coats of paint, the last being of the best white enamel." Faux tile can receive a glazed topcoat for a more tile-like look. Consult books on decorative painting for techniques.

Painting with oil-based enamel (alkyd) is still an option. Avoid really bright whites, which were not available in the early part of the century.

Natural woodwork or wainscoting was customarily finished with shellac or varnish. (To test, dip a cotton swab in denatured alcohol and test in an inconspicuous place; if the finish dissolves, it's shellac. If it doesn't, it's probably varnish.) Shellac tends to darken and crack with age but strips off easily with denatured alcohol or ammonia. (Wear a respirator.) It comes in orange (for that really dipped-in-molasses look) or clear, which is still a little bit amber. Shellac is sensitive to water and alcohol, so it's not the most practical finish, but a few coats of shellac with a topcoat of varnish will give the right look with more durability. (By the way, polyurethane will not work as a topcoat—it won't stick to shellac.)

Existing wallpaper may be in bad shape, and might need to be stripped. Many lovely reproduction wallpapers are being made, but many of them are not appropriate for bathrooms unless coated with varnish. Some may not be stylistically right either—probably nothing terribly formal or really elaborate found its way into the bathroom: an Anglo-Japonesque room-set with seven different patterns would be a bit over the top, even in a Victorian bathroom (though amusing, I admit), and a bathroom of the Arts and Crafts period would be more likely to have something fairly simple.

In 1931, one company was advertising "Cel-Kote" waterproofing, boasting it "can be applied to the finest papers without affecting the color or texture." Washable wall coverings such as Sanitas, Wall-Tex, Koroseal (remember Waldo Semon?), and Salubra were available—these were basically pre-coated with varnish or glaze. Regular papers would be better in a powder room or guest bath. On the other hand, vinyl wallpaper isn't quite the thing either, and most modern washable paper will be coated with vinyl, although some are coated with acrylic. If you put wallpaper in a shower or tub/shower, expect it to peel very soon.

If original stenciling or a hand-painted mural has been uncovered, it would be good to restore it (or replicate it if it's too far gone). Stenciling and murals are also options, if they seem appropriate to the bathroom. (Nineteenth-century and 1920s to '40s baths are more likely to have had elaborate decoration than the ones from the decades in between.)

The biggest problems with tiled walls tend to be dirt, crazing of the glaze, or cracking. It's nice to think of the crazing in the glaze as patina, unless it's allowing water penetration—in fact, you can pay a lot of money for crackle-glazed tiles. For other repairs, see information under "Tubs, Showers, and Flooring." Tile that is too far gone can be refinished using the same method used for fixtures, which is basically high-tech paint. This is fine for white tile; try to avoid using this method on any really special-colored tile. Instructions for repair of structural glass can be found under "Countertops."

There didn't tend to be a whole lot of mirrors in most bathrooms, at least until the 1930s; a mirror on the medicine cabinet and maybe one on another wall or a full-length mirror on the door was about it. Mirrors in bad shape can be re-silvered or replaced.

Compromise Solution

Interestingly enough, you have far more leeway in a Victorian bath, or a 1920s to '40s bath, than in the decades between when things were remarkably white and antiseptic (although not entirely). You might want to think of an all-white bathroom as Zen-like and peaceful, or you could think of it as a blank canvas onto which you can put colored towels and rugs, artwork, plants, and flowers. And generally, it's okay to go a little crazy in a powder room, because no one will be spending large amounts of time in there. But hey, this section is as compromising as I'm ever going to get. Go nuts!

Most people will not notice the difference between drywall and lath-and-plaster, although skim-coat plaster over blueboard is a good compromise. Drywall is a particularly good solution for a badly cracked ceiling: just put up a layer of 1/4- or 3/8-inch drywall right over the plaster. The drywall should have a smooth finish, not a spray texture or that dreadful texture that is so prevalent in modern buildings. It should still be possible to do a faux tile finish with skim-coated drywall. A tin ceiling, if found at all, would likely be in a nineteenth-century bathroom, but if you want to do one anyway, make sure it is well sealed and even back-primed or rust is just about guaranteed.

Latex semigloss is perfectly reasonable for painting walls and ceilings. Flat paint isn't good in bathrooms because of the high moisture content in the room. It is possible to get flat enamel, which will give a matte look and still be easy to keep clean. While off-white to pastels tended to be the colors for the sanitary look, zany colored tile calls for wilder colors of paint. And even white tile won't be hurt by an infusion of color on the walls. It's a good idea to add mildewcide (available at the paint store) to bathroom paint.

Reproduction William de Morgan (an English Arts and Crafts designer) tiles are set into a new subway-tile wainscot in the bathroom of a 1907 Arts and Crafts home.

Varnish or spar varnish is best for unpainted woodwork or wainscoting, or else use shellac with varnish as a topcoat. If you want to use polyurethane, stick with the solvent-based kind: the water based tends to look cloudy when multiple coats are built up.

Stenciling is still an option, either as an all-over pattern for an alternative to wallpaper, as a border, or even as a fake tile wainscot. You can do it yourself (many lovely Arts and Crafts stencils are available, as well as other kinds), or hire a decorative painter. Heck, get a hand-painted mural if you want.

Many varieties of wallpaper are available, from historic reproductions and interpretations to modern vinyl or acrylic-coated wallpapers. Designs range from sublimely beautiful to absolutely hideous. Try to stay near the beautiful end of the range. Here are a few obvious patterns to avoid: cute animals, faux books, cutesy "country" looks, cartoon characters—do you get my drift? And if it's even possible to get this anymore, which I'm not sure it is: avoid flocking. It will make your bathroom look like a Victorian whorehouse.

New wallpaper and borders bring out the colors of this iridescent blue, purple, and black bath in a 1928 Spanish-style house. Black paint on the window sash and medicine cabinet coordinates with the black edge tiles.

Bradbury and Bradbury's Kingfisher frieze highlights the wall above the tile wainscot in a new 6-by-11-foot bath carved out of a former sewing room in a 1909 bungalow. A hexagonal-tile floor with a diaper pattern in the center and a modified Greek key border designed by the homeowners anchors the pedestal sink, toilet, and salvaged footed tub. Mossy green woodwork picks up the floor color.

Purple Anaglypta wallpaper (heavy paper with an embossed design) sends this 1931 yellow, black, and purple bathroom right over the top, where it was headed anyway. It's hard to believe that a bath this zany is hiding inside a staid-looking Tudor residence, which also features a lavender sink in the kitchen.

A previous owner of this 1929 apartment covered all the colored tile in both bathrooms with white tile, leaving just the colored fixtures, which looked wrong. Conveniently, it was done with mastic, making it slightly easier for the current owner to strip it and restore the colored tile. (See photo of restored bath on following page.)

Lincrusta, while not common in period bathrooms, can still make for an interesting wainscoting. It would be best to just paint it, but if doing it up as tooled leather would amuse you, what the heck.

Walls of mirrors were not common until the 1930s and after, although a judicious use of mirrors can make a small bathroom seem larger. If it's a pre-1930 bath, try not to go overboard with them.

There are various ways to go with tile, depending on whether existing tile is being kept and repaired (if possible) or new tile is being installed. Old tile is difficult to demolish, being on a reinforced mortar base, which is probably what led to the widespread preservation of original bathrooms—it was just too much trouble to rip out. It is possible to tile over existing tile if it is firmly attached and the substrate is sound. This is especially useful if you somehow ended up with hideous tile from late in the twentieth century. I would not recommend tiling over original tile. Of course, tiling over the floor will mean raising the toilet and possibly having to trim the bathroom door. If the original tile has to be ripped out (because of rot in the walls, etc.), try to save as much as you can—it can be reused as accents, even if it can't all be saved. (A rule of thumb is that at least 25 percent of it will be damaged.) If you are in a situation where all new tile is being installed, many kinds of appropriate tiles in

(Of course, if your house used to be a Victorian whorehouse, maybe you want to go with that . . .) I must confess here that I have five rolls of black-and-silver flocked brocade wallpaper that I saved from the 1970s—it was in my booth at the Dickens Christmas Fair, where I sold Victorian lingerie, and I am simply unwilling to part with it. Flocked wallpaper is also good for that 1960s tract-house look: gold- or red-flocked wallpaper, swagged gold and crystal hanging lamps, a cultured marble vanity top that resembles caramel saltwater taffy on top of a "Mediterranean"-style cabinet, with some gold-veined mirror tile. Some vinyl papers are very obviously "vinylish," where others are more subtle—try to go with the more subtle ones. Aquatic themes are still appropriate, and tropical themes also seem to lend themselves especially well to the colored-tile bathrooms of the 1920s and '30s. Textured papers such as Anaglypta and

Now restored, the yellow and green original tile sets off the green fixtures the way it was designed to do in 1929 when this apartment was constructed.

Right: Six-inch tiles installed diagonally on the walls give a remarkably contemporary look to a 1932 bath in an Italianate-style house. Pale yellow fixtures sit on a rustic-looking dark blue tile floor.

all price ranges are obtainable: 3-by-6-inch subway tiles, 4-by-4-inch tiles, mosaics, handmade art tiles, tile murals, etc. But think about the year of the house: a nineteenth- or very early-twentieth century house could have Minton tiles or William de Morgan reproductions, or it might just have white subway tiles. In fact, white or off-white tiles are a safe choice in just about any decade. A house from 1913 would most likely have white tiles. A house from 1926 is far more likely to have lavender and green or some other wild color combination, although it might just as easily have white. A house from 1929 into the 1930s might have wild color combinations, art tile, or structural glass. (See "Countertops" for structural glass alternatives.) Cement backer board and thin-set mortar are certainly a reasonable alternative to a mortar bed. Backer board should have plastic sheeting or building felt (tar paper) behind it to prevent moisture intrusion into the walls. And what should you do if you absolutely hate the existing tile and it's original? Time to re-parameterize. Go with it. Go over the top with it. If it's pink and blue (a combination I particularly detest), just make it the pinkest bathroom on earth. Paint a pink flamingo mural; bring in a palm tree, get towels with flamingos embroidered on them, buy blue liquid soap, use pink light bulbs. Or add black accents—black will work wonders with almost any color. If the tile is not original, you can always have it refinished, bearing in mind that refinishing means basically painting it. On the other hand, it means you'll never have to clean the grout again.

A tile medallion in gold, black, teal, and turquoise is set in a field of red tiles in a 1932 bath.

DECOR ISSUES

In the nineteenth century, bathrooms were decorated in rather the same way as the bedrooms from which the fixtures had migrated. They had paneling, carpet, stained glass, wallpaper, artwork, and even pieces of furniture. Toward the end of the nineteenth century and into the early twentieth, sanitation took over, and bathrooms became much more austere.

With the coming of colored tile and fixtures in the 1920s, there was a trend toward more decoration. But even the most austere bathrooms generally had towels, rugs, used-towel baskets, and curtains.

Turkish toweling (terry cloth) was favored, but flat woven towels were also used. Turkish towels were white (or unbleached) up until about 1928, although they often had colored borders. Sometimes the borders were patterned, often with aquatic themes like seashells, lighthouses, ships, or fish. In 1928 colored towels were introduced, probably in reaction to all the colored tile. Even so, they only came in pastels such as pink, gold, blue, green, and yellow. Egyptian cotton makes the best towels. Flat woven towels, embroidered, appliqued, or with lace edging, were favored as guest towels. Bins of metal wire for used towels (so they could dry out) were a common accessory.

Rugs were used to take the cold edge off tile floors. In the Victorian period, these were often oriental rugs, but by the twentieth century, plain rugs were used, either flat woven or with a pile, occasionally with a colored border. Mostly these were cotton, so they could be laundered.

Curtains were used on bathroom windows both

*An antique scale decorates one bathroom
in the 1899 Dunsmuir House.*

*Pinkish green art tile by the Muresque Tile Company
with various decorative tiles scattered through it is laid
in a random pattern resembling stonework around a
green bathtub in a 1930 Spanish-style home.*

for privacy if the glass was clear and for decoration and softening if the glass was obscure. A 1924 issue of *House and Garden* made the following recommendation:

Curtains should be of some material that looks fresh and crisp and launders well. Marquisette and voile are durable, wash well, and do not pull out of shape as easily as net. But they are apt to get thick looking after repeated washings and have not the crisp looking appearance of dotted swiss, which is an ideal material for bathroom curtains. It can be trimmed with rickrack braid to match the color of the dots or simply hemstitched in color. Rubberized taffeta, which comes in many delightful colors, makes effective bathroom curtains, and for a window too small for hangings, glazed chintz is the smartest thing to use, made into a roller shade.

*A rose by any other name is still pink, so these homeowners went with it and added pink wallpaper
(with a border that echoes the motif of the art-glass window), blue accents, Art Deco light fixtures, and a
round aquarium (thus fulfilling the goldfish requirement), rather than ripping out this 1925 bathroom.*

A lot of bathroom curtains had ruffles on the edges or hems. The ubiquitous curtain rod of the Arts and Crafts period (and beyond) was the 3/8-inch brass rod with barrel brackets.

Furniture often found its way into bathrooms that were big enough for it: small tables, dressing tables, chairs, and freestanding cabinets. The style of this furniture didn't necessarily have anything to do with the style of the bathroom.

It is also possible to transform a bathroom of a later period simply with decor. For instance, a bathroom from the 1950s with yellow or blue tile that is just too good to rip out can be magically transformed into an Art Deco bathroom simply by replacing the sink with a pedestal model, putting in some Art Deco light fixtures, and adding black accents such as towels, rugs, a black border on the curtains, and black accessories.

One of the best ways to patch damaged tile is to fill in the hole with a tile mural, although this mural is original to this very feminine pink bathroom.

rug, although a priceless antique would probably not be a good idea—perhaps a nice reproduction instead. Plain rugs are still easy to come by. Most modern bathroom rugs have latex backing that renders them nonslip; a rug that doesn't will require a pad. If there's room for furniture, bring in whatever seems appropriate. Again, the bathroom is not the place for rare antiques, but a little table, small cabinet, or chair might be a fine addition.

Bathroom curtains need to be washable and able to stand up to steam. Simple curtains of muslin, linen, broadcloth, and such, usually with a rod pocket or occasionally with rings, are fine in most periods. If you want to take *House and Garden's* advice, voile (a sheer cotton), marquisette (a mesh fabric—basically mosquito netting), and dotted swiss (a sheer cotton with a woven pattern of small dots) are still available. Rubberized taffeta probably isn't.

Many curtains had ruffles, so do that if you want, but I personally don't condone ruffles or dotted swiss. Bathrooms usually didn't have really elaborate window treatments: no molded cornice boards, no tassels, no floor-length velvet drapes lined with silk (not that this wouldn't be amusing). Barrel brackets in various configurations and 3/8-inch brass rods are still obtainable, though probably not at the local fabric store. (See "Resources.")

Obsessive Restoration (Decor)

For the truly obsessive, use only white or unbleached towels in any pre-1928 bathroom. It is still possible to get colored woven borders, and aquatic themes are still quite popular. Plain towels are fine also. After 1928, stick with the pastels mentioned above, assuming they go with the bathroom. Wire baskets for used towels are hard to find nowadays, because who wants to look at a heap of damp towels? Antiques dealers are the best bet for this. A nineteenth-century bathroom is the place for an oriental

Left: White linen towels with tatted edging hang on a towel rack at the Dunsmuir House.
Middle: Pink huck toweling with an inset lace border picks up the pink tile edging in a bath at the 1901 Stimson-Green Mansion.
Right: Red, black, and gold tiles imported from Korea line the walls of a powder room in a 1932 Spanish home.
Jacquard towels on a black towel bar harmonize with the tile colors.

Compromise Solution

Towels come in a wide variety of colors now, so if you want color, go for it. (A hint: If you're trying to match the tile color, it really helps to take a tile sample with you to the store.) Both antique and new guest towels are also available, although you still won't be able to get anyone to use them. Many lines of towels are color coordinated with rugs, toilet seat covers, and various other accessories. Instead of towel baskets, we now have laundry hampers made of things like wicker, cane, metal, or plastic. Stick with the natural materials.

A nineteenth-century bathroom (or even a twentieth-century one) can still have an oriental rug, but perhaps this is the place

A used-towel basket sits beneath a marble vanity with a shield-shaped mirror and nickel-plated legs. An "elephant trunk" embossed wash-out toilet bowl is on the right. To the left of the mirror is a wall-mounted whisk-broom holder. (Courtesy of Vintage Plumbing.)

A stepped Deco stool sits next to a built-in tile-topped chest in an 8-by-10-foot blue-and-black bath, one of four in this 1929 Mediterranean-style home.

*This very large bathroom at the 1899 Dunsmuir House has plenty of room for
a wicker chaise lounge, should one wish to stretch out before or after bathing.*

for that machine-woven polypropylene reproduction. Rugs made especially for the bathroom are sold in both cotton and synthetics with latex backing that gives them nonslip properties. If there's room, it is still possible to bring in furniture. Many reproductions that fit in quite well are available through catalogs and at stores. And, heck, if you've always wanted a sofa in your bathroom and there is room for it, get one.

Curtains haven't changed much either. It is now possible to have almost any fabric "vinylized" to be waterproof, especially good for windows over a tub or in a shower. Otherwise, any washable fabric will be fine. Curtain rods should be fairly simple, though: café rods, rods with barrel brackets, etc. Wooden shutters,

Plants, a basket of towels, and a modern soap pump bring color and softness to this pink bathroom.

Roman shades, roller shades, and venetian blinds are also options. Try to stay away from vertical blinds or mini-blinds—so late twentieth-century.

In the twenty-first century, we have many items that weren't around in earlier periods, like liquid soap pumps, special rugs that fit around the base of the toilet, and so forth. And while old bathrooms generally didn't have artwork in them, we may want that. Stick to inexpensive prints, as steam and water are not good for most artwork. On the other hand, if you want to bring in art pottery, it should be fine. Other accessories like baskets, candles, plants, and fresh flowers are welcome touches.

Layout & Design

The first bathroom I remember was in my childhood home in Indianapolis, which was built in the 1920s. It was 5 by 5 feet, and it served three adults and three children. It had a five-foot tub with a window over it on the back wall, a toilet on the left-hand wall, a sink on the right, and a white hexagonal-tile floor. My father added a shower to the tub, which didn't originally have one.

A very typical bathroom layout has the tub on one side in a niche with a lowered ceiling, the toilet and sink on the other side, and one window at the end, all in a space ranging from a minimum of about 5 by 6 feet to a maximum of about 7 by 9 feet. Sometimes a stall shower is installed at the end of the bathtub by the door. This 1920s bath also has the characteristic hexagonal-tile floors, white fixtures, and white tile found in most bathrooms between 1900 and 1925.

In the 1970s, I rented a flat in a 1910 duplex. The bathroom was five feet wide and six feet deep. The toilet was on the back wall on the left, a claw-foot tub ran parallel to the right-hand wall, and a round wall-hung sink was mounted on the left-hand wall almost directly over the toilet bowl in such a way that to sit on the toilet one had to slide sideways under the sink.

Typical bath layouts.

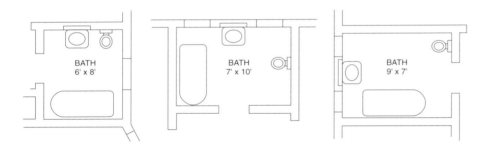

If your bathroom is bigger than either of these, you're lucky, because most are quite small.

If you are restoring an original bathroom and don't plan to change anything, then layout will not be a concern. However, if you are starting from scratch, adding another bath, or trying to make an existing bath function better, then layout will become an issue. Most historic bathrooms tend to be small by modern standards, though not all of them. Still, 5 by 7 feet or 6 by 8 feet is a fairly common size, and a powder room or half-bath can be even smaller.

ARCHAEOLOGY

Bathrooms are the second most-likely room to have been altered, after the kitchen. Yet a remarkable number of bathrooms remain intact in their original condition, probably because the functional requirements haven't changed that much. Some bathrooms may have been altered in various ways yet retain much of their original fabric. It is not always possible to figure out how they have been altered, but there are clues. Sometimes a little judicious exploratory demolition may be in order. Fixtures have often been replaced or moved, usually sinks and toilets, bathtubs far less often. Wall-hung sinks may have been replaced with vanities. Examine the wall closely for paint "ghosts" or evidence of plaster patching. Toilets often get replaced because of cracked tanks or bowls, broken tank lids, or just the urge to modernize. (Look inside the tank lid to see if it's stamped with a manufacture date.) Toilets are also sometimes replaced with low-flow models. Separate tap faucets may have been replaced with mixing models (and if they have plastic handles, you know they're not old). Replacement of hardware, light fixtures, cabinets, or floor coverings is also common. Putting vinyl or linoleum over ceramic tile or wood seems to be pretty common—pry up a corner to see. Cabinet doors were often changed to modern "slab" doors. And that sliding aluminum window is probably not original, although if you're lucky, the wooden window that was removed is still lying around somewhere. A "faux tile" plaster wainscot may have disappeared under multiple layers of paint—look underneath the sink or behind the toilet for evidence. One of the best ways to get a sense of what the original bathroom might have been like is to visit other historic homes in your area, either on house tours or at real-estate open houses. After seeing a lot of original bathrooms, a sense of what they were like will start to emerge, and in particular, what they were like in your neck of the woods.

One layout issue is the position of the bathroom within the house. Bathrooms were usually located off a hallway—to save space or for various other reasons—and sometimes ended up in weird places. For instance, many homes that didn't originally have indoor plumbing may have the only bath out on the utility porch, or shoehorned into a closet. One layout very common to bungalows was to place the bath between two bedrooms with access only from the bedrooms (although sometimes there was a third door from the hallway). Then there is bath placement that is just plain bad, for instance, off the living or dining room (yuck!), or off the kitchen (which can be mitigated by being around a corner or through a really short hallway). Another really annoy-

Sinks were sometimes installed in bedrooms or closets, as this wall-hung cast-iron sink in the closet of a 1910 house demonstrates.

ing placement is to have the only bath upstairs, with nothing on the ground floor. Try to fit in a half-bath or at least a toilet on the ground floor in this case. There may or may not be anything to be done about bad placement—I rejected one otherwise lovely bungalow for purchase because its only bathroom was off the dining room and there was no way to fix it.

When indoor plumbing first appeared, it was a novelty to have even one bathroom, let alone more than one. Today we prefer the equation "one bedroom = one bathroom." This may not always be possible in a small house without adding on. But sometimes

The unusual layout of this 1928 bathroom includes a "wet room," which contains both the bathtub and a showerhead on the opposite wall, with a floor drain. (See photo on page 147.)

space can be found by using a closet, annexing a closet, or reconfiguring some walls. A half-bath is obviously easier to fit in than a full bath. Possibly a small room like a study, sewing room, or enclosed porch can be taken over. Having a stall shower instead of a tub often means a smaller space can be utilized. Try to resist the urge to take a third or fourth bedroom and make it over into a huge, luxurious bathroom—this is rarely an appropriate thing to do. Sometimes putting one of the fixtures somewhere else (like the toilet in a closet, or the sink in the bedroom) will make it work. On the other hand, putting the shower in the bedroom (and I have actually seen this) is probably not a good idea. If a closet is being taken over for another bath, alternate closet space will have to be found. Code requirements may also figure in, since certain clearances between walls and fixtures, and in front of fixtures, are required.

A replacement toilet sits on a herringbone-tiled floor in a toilet room (or W. C.), which is separate from the rest of the bathroom. These rooms can be a little claustrophobic, so it helps to have a window.

Rearrangement of an existing bath might make it more workable, but keep in mind that it is expensive to move plumbing. Sinks are the easiest things to move, while toilets and tubs are much more difficult. Adding a second sink is not too difficult if there is room. Sometimes just replacing the fixtures with smaller ones will work wonders. Many space-saving fixtures are available, both salvaged and new: small sinks, corner sinks, four-foot tubs, extra-small toilets, corner showers, even corner toilets. In a bathroom with three doors, it may be possible to close off one of them to gain more space. Or sometimes using a pocket door (that slides into the wall) instead of a swinging door will make the space workable. The addition of cabinets or using recessed space between wall studs will increase storage options.

A large recessed medicine cabinet with hinged mirrors is paired with a large cantilevered shelf (which could also function as a dressing table) in the Arts and Crafts–style Riordan House in Flagstaff, Arizona.

Set in a board-and-batten-paneled bath, a coat rack and long-legged cabinet provide storage next to a pedestal-style Roman tub.

The cat box question is a serious one, at least for those of us who have cats. The bathroom is a practical place for it, especially with the advent of flushable clumping litter, but it's not a fun place to have it. Perhaps building an extra bathroom for the cats is the answer. If there's both a tub and a stall shower and no one ever takes baths, keeping it in the tub will at least keep the flying kitty litter contained. The half-bath off the utility porch (if there is one) might be a better location, and here's a situation where a wall-hung sink is useful: the cat box can go underneath. I don't really have a good answer, I just dream of a self-cleaning cat bathroom.

Almost any kind of layout is possible, but there are four that are common. The first is the one-wall layout, where all the fixtures are arrayed along one wall in a long, narrow room (as narrow as four and a half feet). This is economical in terms of plumbing, since it is all in one wall. The second is the corridor layout, with fixtures located on opposite walls, usually sink and toilet on one wall, tub and stall shower (if any) on the other. This layout seems to be especially common in bungalows. The third is the U-shaped bathroom, with fixtures on three walls in a square room. This layout requires plumbing in all three walls, making it more expensive in plumbing terms. The fourth is the L-shaped layout, which usually has the bathtub along the short wall. All the plumbing can be in one wall in this layout also. But many variations on these are possible.

Many of our bathroom items aren't that big (toothbrush, shaving equipment, makeup, soap, etc.), so recessed storage between wall studs is a good idea. It's useful to keep extra toilet paper where it can be reached by someone sitting on the toilet. A wall-hung cabinet over the back of the toilet is extremely useful anyway, and can be made deep enough for this purpose. Sometimes there is an existing cabinet, or space for one, at the end of the tub. Freestanding cabinets can also be useful in this regard. Obviously vanities provide far more storage than wall-hung or pedestal sinks.

A common layout sets the tub and toilet on one wall and the sink on the other, as shown in this 1920s yellow and green bath.

Bordered in morning glories, a green-and-black-tile wainscot dresses up a proto-typical layout in a modest late-1920s bungalow. At that time in the 1920s, even small houses began to have separate stall showers like this one.

my life, I slipped and fell in the bathtub. One of my first thoughts was why hadn't I installed a grab bar? Then my mother, who is getting on in years, came to visit. She found it nearly impossible to get in and out of my bathtub in order to take a shower. The combination of water, electricity, and hard, slick surfaces makes bathrooms inherently dangerous, but more so for those who are physically challenged in some way (which might be you when you have the stomach flu). Give some thought to incorporating safety in ways that don't compromise the historic feel of the room.

FENG SHUI

Feng shui (the Chinese art of placement) is far too complex to go into here, but there is a *feng shui* rule that applies to the bathroom. In brief, *feng shui* is the art of making *chi* (life force—think *Star Wars*, "May the Force be with you") bounce around your house like a ball in a pinball machine before exiting. Harnessing the *chi* brings balance, harmony, prosperity, and good luck to the house's occupants. The rule is: always leave the toilet seat down and the lid closed; otherwise the *chi* will go right down the toilet. The women in your household will be grateful also. *Feng shui* rules also discourage the currently popular "master suite" with a bathroom off the master bedroom.

This is not really the place to address ADA (Americans with Disabilities Act) issues, except to say that many historic bathrooms are not very accessible. But wider doorways, roll-in showers, and especially grab bars may be a good idea for everyone, considering the aging population. I never gave much thought to any of this until recently, when, for the first time in

OLD AND NEW

Adding new cabinets, windows, fixtures, and such to an existing bathroom requires matching door and drawer styles, old moldings, hardware, and so forth. More information on this can be found under the individual categories. New moldings can be made to match existing ones. The most expensive part of this is having a knife made to match the molding profile. This can now be done with lasers, which has made it a little less expensive.

The trickier part of melding old and new is to make sure the new parts are at least historically probable, even if they might not have been there originally. For instance, adding a vanity to a bathroom that didn't originally have one is fine, if it's a fairly simple painted cabinet, but a fumed oak vanity with hammered copper pulls is simply not historically plausible; putting in a "Victorian-style" acrylic whirlpool tub (and there is such a thing), well, it just makes one shudder. And how many times has a magazine article quoted a design professional saying something like, "We wanted to blend the old with some contemporary touches." Don't do that—you end up with something that is neither here nor there and is disrespectful to an old house.

The 1932 version of a grab bar is rendered in metal and glass.

In the 1920s, many soap dishes also included grab bars.

STARTING FROM SCRATCH

Perhaps the existing bathroom is so dreadful that all you can do is rip it out and start over, or maybe you are adding an additional bathroom. An existing bathroom will still have things to be worked around, such as doors, windows, plumbing locations and such, and adding a bath by utilizing an existing closet or other room will have similar (or even more) constraints. On the other hand, a bath in an addition will have fewer restraints. The main thing in a new bath is that it should stylistically harmonize with the existing bath(s), or at least with the house, if you are ripping out the only bathroom. So, in a house from the 1920s with colored-tile bathrooms, the new bath should also have colored tile. On the other hand, if the existing baths are white, the new one should be white. A modest bungalow should not have a huge bathroom lined in marble, whereas a grand house might actually be able to support that, if that's what the other bathrooms are like.

It becomes even trickier, if, for instance, the bathrooms in a nineteenth-century house were remodeled in the 1930s. I would not necessarily condone ripping out the 1930s baths to replace them with something more historically appropriate, but perhaps a new bath might be based on nineteenth-century

This 1928 bath has an interesting layout with a separate "wet room" containing the tub and shower (at left). An added bath in a house like this ought to have colored tile, as this one does, though not necessarily the same color. (The other original bath in this home is iridescent blue-purple and black; see bathtub on page 140.)

designs. A new bath may allow for two sinks, more storage and counter space, and other things we demand in the twenty-first century. There is even historic precedent (in grander houses and apartments) for the attached dressing rooms or walk-in closets that are popular now in new construction. On the other hand, don't put in a fireplace.

It may be helpful to do some research about historic bathroom layouts. Reprints of catalogs from mail-order house-plan companies (of the appropriate period) are particularly useful because they contain floor plans that provide a feel for what kinds of layouts were common, or they might furnish ideas useful to your particular situation.

Assessing Your Needs and Dealing with Professionals

*N*obody expects the Spanish Inquisition!"
—*Monty Python's Flying Circus*

The restoration of this Muresque-tile sunken shower definitely called for professional help but was well worth it. This 1930 bathroom is a masterpiece of amazing tile work, including landscape tiles, a three-dimensional fish, and an art-tile light fixture. A beamed ceiling adds to the rustic look.

Before embarking on a restoration or a new bathroom, it's important to look inside. Not inside the bathroom, but inside yourself. A lot of questions need to be answered before you ever hire a contractor or purchase a fixture. The test will not be graded, so answer the questions honestly. Do you like to take baths, or do you mostly shower? Do you have kids? How old are they? Are you sharing the bathroom with others? Are you a slob or a neatnik? Do you consider the bathroom a retreat or just a place to get clean? Do you like everything stored behind closed doors, or out in the open? How do you feel about exposed plumbing? Do you care about impressing your friends or neighbors? If you have brass hardware, do you care if it tarnishes? Will you polish it if it does?

Do you want to do all or some of the work yourself? Do you have the skills, or do you think you can learn them? Do you have the time? (It will take longer than you think.) If you are redoing the only bathroom, how are you going to cope without one? Do you know which things to leave to professionals? Do you want to act as your own general contractor? Do you have the time to do that? Or would you be better off working to earn the money to pay someone else to oversee it? What is your budget? What happens if you go over it (and you will)? Are you decisive or do you change your mind every five minutes? If you have other people in the house, they must also answer these questions.

It is entirely possible to spend lots of money and not do it intelligently. Knowing what you need and also what is appropriate to a historic bathroom will help. It will also greatly decrease the number of decisions you have to make. For example, you won't have to decide between all two thousand kinds of cabinet hardware (or whatever) in a catalog, only the fifteen or twenty that are historically accurate.

DUST IN THE WIND(OW)

Most people are not prepared for the stress of renovation. There are seemingly endless decisions to be made, even for a period bathroom, and eventually you will find yourself in the middle of a heated argument about hardware (or something) with either the contractor or your significant other or both. After a very short time, the novelty of using a portable toilet in the backyard or washing your hair in the kitchen sink will wear off and you will be really irritable. Everything you own will be covered with plaster dust, no matter how much effort is made to keep it out of the rest of the house, and you will begin to question your own sanity. The one valuable thing you forgot to put away for safekeeping will get broken. Then you will come down with the flu. At that point you will begin to fantasize about moving into a brand-new condominium and giving up this old-house madness altogether.

There is a particular form of stress attached to restoring or redoing a period bathroom, and that is overcoming the objections of the people you will be dealing with in order to get what you want. You will constantly hear the following phrases: "Nobody makes those anymore," "You can't do it that way," "Why would you want that?" "Nobody uses _____ anymore," "Why don't you tear out all of this plaster and put up drywall?" "We have to take this down to the studs and start over," and "But a whirlpool tub will increase the resale value."

Then there is your family. Even if you and possibly your significant other are in agreement (and you might as well start counseling immediately if you're not, and possibly even if you are), it is entirely possible that your family, your siblings, your friends, your real-estate agent, and/or your neighbors will believe that you have completely lost your mind. As things start to go wrong or the project starts to go over budget, they will become more vocal and you will begin to wonder if perhaps they are right. Do your best to ignore them. Try to remember that you are only the caretaker of this house, and that you are doing the right thing for the house and for future generations. Hopefully this book will give you the ammunition needed to stand firm in the face of these objections in order to get the bathroom you have in mind.

Restoration is messy, as in this 1929 bath that had been tiled over in white, shown here in the middle of restoration (see finished bath on page 79).

CREWS AID

Even if you are doing the entire renovation yourself, there are still many people to deal with. You may not be dealing with every one of these people, but you'll definitely be dealing with some of them. Try to keep in mind at all times that they are working for you, since they will sometimes lose sight of that fact. Also bear in mind that many of them have their own agendas, often involving parting you from large amounts of your money (not that they are necessarily dishonest, merely less than objective). It's important to educate yourself so you know where it is appropriate to spend a lot of money and where it isn't. Even if you have a lot of money, there is no need to spend it foolishly. There are good, bad, and mediocre people in every field, so be sure to get references and referrals and check them out. Also keep in mind that there are very few people who know or understand period bathrooms, or I wouldn't be writing this book. It may be more difficult to find the right people for your project than it would be for a remodel in a contemporary tract house.

ARCHITECTS

Unless you are planning an addition or some really major structural changes, you probably don't need an architect. An architect will argue otherwise, of course. There are some architects who understand historic buildings, but knowledge of historic building styles or even building itself does not seem to be part of modern architectural training, which seems to emphasize self-expression over anything else.

If you are going to hire an architect, I would certainly interview several. Ask to see pictures of other bathrooms they've done. Assess whether they will be receptive to your wants and needs. If you feel you are

A project like this stepped bathtub niche requires not only a talented tile installer but also a good contractor to frame the niche properly.

being talked down to or if they seem like they have an agenda of their own, keep looking.

There are architects who specialize in historic preservation projects, though this won't necessarily mean they know anything about period bathrooms. Your local preservation organization, historical society, or even the local planning or building department may be able to give you referrals. You can hire an architect to oversee the whole project, or you can hire one just for the design and drawings. You can even hire one by the hour for feedback about your own ideas. Sometimes an architect can be useful for coming up with a creative solution to a difficult layout problem. Using an architect will add to the cost of the project, especially if he/she is overseeing it.

Another option is a design/build contractor, where the design and building functions are combined in one company. This is often a less-expensive alternative than hiring an architect, and can be a good alternative, especially for projects that are fairly simple.

CONTRACTORS AND SUBCONTRACTORS

Unless you plan to do every single thing yourself, you will probably be hiring contractors. You can hire a general contractor to take charge of the entire project, who will hire subcontractors (plumbers, electricians, carpenters, tile setters, etc.) as needed for various specialty jobs. Some general contractors also have their own crews who cover all or most of the trades needed. A general contractor will put a mark-up on the work of the subcontractors, so you can save money by acting as the general contractor and hiring subcontractors directly. However, this means you need to have the time and also the knowledge of the sequence in which things need to be done in order to schedule the subs. It can be hard to get cooperation from the subs, who tend to be loyal to the contractors who give them steady work, making you the last one on the list. You also need to have the time to be on the job site to make sure things are going as planned and to make decisions, so it's not a good idea for someone with a full-time job to be their own general contractor. If you are hiring a general contractor or a subcontractor, all the usual caveats apply: ask for references, get at least three bids (in writing), make sure the bids are for the same scope of work, have a written contract that clearly spells everything out in great detail, and so forth. I would recommend getting a few books on the subject from a library or bookstore, or peruse one of the many articles on this subject to be found in various home magazines.

Here are a few other words of wisdom based on my experience. I always hear stories of a mythical contractor, usually an older man who works alone, has superb craftsmanship, and doesn't charge very much. Where is this guy? How come I've never run across him? If you've actually found him, lucky you. The reality is closer to this: mostly, you get what you pay for. Which doesn't mean you should pay for more than you need. A contractor who specializes in meticulous restoration (and charges accordingly) may not be what you need if you're building an addition.

A contracting firm (as opposed to a one- or two-person business) may send someone to present the bid who is basically a salesperson. That person may be extremely personable and will assure you that, of course, it can all be done on schedule and on budget. But this is not who you will be dealing with on a day-to-day basis. Ask to meet the foreman and the crew who will be working on your project. Go to a job site where they are working now and observe the crew. You will be involved in a fairly intimate relationship with these people, so it will be much less stressful if you actually like them. Talk to the person who will be in charge of your project. Is that person respectful or are you hearing a few of the telltale phrases detailed earlier in this chapter? Is that person receptive to old homes or is there an underlying attitude that newer is always better, that existing things are not worth saving? What radio station is the crew listening to? If you are going to be home during the project, will that station drive you nuts? (Someone I know writes "homeowner gets to choose radio station" into the contract.) You should go with your gut instinct about the crew, because if you don't get along with them now, things are not going to improve later.

Knowledge is power. The best thing to do is to educate yourself as much as you can about the construction process. You don't need to be able to do everything, but it helps to understand the various ways it could be done. It helps to know the jargon as well. And remember, a contractor's primary motivation is money. Once you make the final payment, they're gone, whether the job is actually finished or not.

All that being said, don't be a bad client. Many people don't visualize very well, and often after the contractor has built exactly what they said they wanted, they don't like it and then expect it to be redone at no charge. So try to be very clear about what you want, and use visual aids such as models or computer-assisted design to get a clearer idea of what it's going to look like. Try not to change your mind every five minutes (or if that's the sort of person you are, warn the contractor ahead of time), because changes cost money. Some changes are unavoidable, like opening up a wall and finding an unexpected plumbing stack, but some changes are due to homeowner indecisiveness. Try to stick to your decisions once they're made, yet be flexible when it's necessary. Keep some perspective, too—the earth will not stop turning on its axis just because the porcelain faucet handles don't match the tile color to absolute perfection.

ELECTRICIANS

The good thing about electricians is that they tend to be a little more focused than most subs because they realize electricity can kill you if you don't pay attention. They seem to fall into two categories: those who are willing to "fish" wires through small holes (which is tedious and time-consuming) and those who prefer to open up several stud bays and let someone else patch the plaster later. You can save a lot of money by fishing the wires yourself and having the electrician make the final connections. Try to find someone who has experience with old houses and is able to deal with existing knob-and-tube wiring. It is not necessary to rip it all out if it is still in good condition.

PLUMBERS

There is no one you will need more in redoing a bathroom. Any plumber can install a new toilet, but to deal with old fixtures and faucets you need someone who understands and has experience with them, and is willing to possibly rebuild rather than replace them. You need someone who can recognize a lead closet bend, or is willing to install a salvaged bathtub. A plumbing company that has been in business for a long time (for instance, if their advertising says "Established 1902," that might be a good sign) may be a source for this sort of plumber. Referrals from the local salvage yard can be useful as well. This sort of person may not be necessary for pipe replacement or for a bathroom with all-new plumbing and fixtures.

CARPENTERS

If you are doing a lot of the work yourself, you may only need to hire a carpenter for complex framing or finish work (installing windows, cabinets, trim, and moldings). Finish carpentry has a different skill set than framing, and not all carpenters will be good at both. Unpainted woodwork and cabinets require a higher level of finish carpentry because mistakes can't be rectified with filler and paint. Also, a bathroom needs to have the highest level of workmanship (in all the trades) because people spend a lot of time sitting in there, giving ample opportunity for examining the workmanship up close and at length.

CABINETMAKERS

A period bathroom may involve custom cabinets. All the magazines will tell you that this is the most expensive option, and it can be, especially if you go crazy with custom finishes or elaborate door styles. But for the simple cabinets that are appropriate for most bathrooms, it can be a less-expensive alternative.

The magic question to ask of potential cabinetmakers is, "Can you make flush inset doors?" If the reply is some variation on "Nobody makes those anymore," then keep looking. If the answer is yes, proceed to ask about cabinets without toe kicks, mortised hinges, and even wooden drawer runners. If the answer is still yes, that may be the right person for the job. I have had better luck using those who just build cabinets, and not those who would prefer to be building elaborate furniture with inlays of rare South American hardwoods; they may be bored building plain Shaker-door cabinets.

There are also large custom-cabinet companies that ship nationwide. Their products are available directly to consumers or through kitchen and bath showrooms and designers. They range in price from fairly reasonable to really expensive.

Marble slabs like those lining this master bath in a 1939 Moderne house are best installed by professionals. The walls are original to the house, but the floor was rotted and had to be replaced with new marble in a complementary color. The pivoting cup holder shows only a flat chrome face when turned back into its recessed niche.

PAINTERS

Painting is one of the easiest things to do yourself, but if you are going to hire painters, remember that they will paint anything that has not been removed or masked off, so take off or mask all of the hardware, light fixtures, switch plates, and anything else you don't want painted. Don't wait for them to do it. If they are spraying the paint, it's a good idea to remove furniture, rugs, and such from adjacent rooms, and make sure the bathroom is well masked off to prevent over-spray from drifting anywhere else. Hope to find a painter who is obsessively neat, but if not, it's

TILE SETTERS

It takes a very talented installer to plan the kind of extremely complex layout found in this 1929 Malibu-tile bath. The steps, curves, and different kinds of tile greatly increase the difficulty but also make for a really fabulous bathroom. The arched windows (one over the toilet also) add to the charm of this room in what is really a rather modest Spanish-style bungalow.

If you are using ceramic tile in the bathroom, the tile setter is almost as important as the plumber. If you are doing very simple tile (especially a new installation), you won't necessarily need a high-end installer who specializes in really elaborate installations or restoration. On the other hand, if you are trying to patch or save existing historic tile, then you will want a specialist. Tile setting is messy, and a good tile setter will mask off cabinets and other areas to keep off mortar and grout. Tile dealers are usually a good source of referrals.

FLOORING INSTALLERS

Usually the flooring store has installers with whom they contract, or they have their own employees for installation. Installing linoleum is different from installing vinyl, so make sure the person they send has experience with linoleum, and that they also have experience with inlay if that is involved.

good to know that paint spatters are easy to remove from ceramic tile, metal, and glass.

Decorative painters are a separate category. If you want to have a mural painted or a faux finish put on the wall, this is who you need. Ask to see a portfolio, and be clear about what you want. If wallpaper is involved, you may also need to hire a paperhanger. Usually the place where you bought the wallpaper will be a good source of referrals.

INTERIOR DESIGNERS

If you are not confident about designing your own bathroom, you may want to employ an interior designer. She or he can help with layout and space-planning issues, choosing various bathroom elements, as well as decor. A designer also will have access to products that are available only "to the trade" and not to the general public. Interior designers work in various ways: hourly, for a flat fee, or by adding a mark-up onto things they purchase for you. As with other professionals, many designers may have little understanding of period bathrooms and may suggest things that are currently stylish but inappropriate for an old house. Kitchen and bath designers deal specifically with kitchens and baths and are often found at kitchen/bath showrooms, cabinet companies, home centers, or through design/build contractors. Be aware that those employed by showrooms are likely to want to sell you the products carried by that showroom. As with other design professionals, they may or may not have much knowledge of historic bathrooms but can be helpful in solving layout and other problems.

BUILDING INSPECTORS

If you are redoing your bathroom with permits, you (or your contractor) will be dealing with the building department and whatever version of the building code has been adopted in your area, with a few state and local regulations thrown in for good measure. The building code is concerned with health and safety issues, and is continually changed in an effort to prevent building-related accidents. It is aimed primarily at new construction, and thus causes many problems for historic buildings. There are many things in historic buildings that met code when they were built but do not meet today's code. Sometimes there have been improvements in technology that make sense to incorporate (grounded outlets, GFCIs), but other things do not (like mandating fluorescent lights to save energy, when far more energy could be saved by mandating insulation retrofits). Left alone, many things in historic houses that do not meet modern code are "grandfathered" in, meaning you don't have to bring them up to current code. Trying to make an old house comply with modern code can be difficult, and whatever latitude you may get to do it in ways that do not impact the historic look will be entirely at the whim of your local building inspector.

Some states have adopted a Historic Building Code or something like it. This is a code with more flexibility and sensitivity to historic buildings. Unfortunately, to be eligible to use it, your house usually needs to be on some register: the National Register of Historic Places, the State Historic Register, or your local Historic Register. It is certainly worth looking into if your home qualifies. (Call your State Historic Preservation Office for information.) Some states have gone a bit farther and passed "rehabilitation" codes that apply to all old buildings, regardless of recognition or status. If your state doesn't have this, it might be something to lobby for.

Otherwise, it is entirely up to the local jurisdiction and the building inspector in particular whether you get to replace your windows with historically correct single-glazed panes, hide a GFCI inside a cabinet, or put your toilet an inch closer to the tub than is technically allowed. Some cities and inspectors are remarkably flexible about this sort of thing, while others are infuriatingly obsessed with the letter rather than the spirit of the code. Some inspectors will go over the work of do-it-yourselfers with a particularly fine-toothed comb, while others will give a homeowner a lot more leeway. Some building departments will allow a contractor to get a permit using a pencil sketch on the back of a napkin while requiring you as the homeowner to submit a full set of blueprints, but sometimes it's the other way around.

If you are putting on an addition or making exterior changes, you may also need to deal with a planning or zoning board, a design review commission, or, if your house is a landmark or historically significant, a landmarks or historic preservation board. You may also have to deal with a neighborhood association. Politics can be involved here, so tread carefully. It's good to get the neighbors on your side ahead of time. On the other hand, if you're proposing to build a three-story addition two feet from the property line that will cut off all sunlight to your neighbor's backyard, you'd better start rethinking that right now.

SALVAGE YARDS

If you want old stuff, eventually you'll end up at a salvage yard. There you will find much old stuff that is rusted, warped, or damaged, at semi-outrageous prices. The stuff that is actually in decent condition will command even more outrageous prices. However, if you want to buy a vintage cage shower or old ceramic towel-bar holders, a salvage yard is the place to go. Some things at a salvage yard will be cheaper than their new equivalents, and for things that have no new equivalent, a salvage yard may be one of the only sources. You will generally get a lower price on these things at estate sales or through private parties, but that isn't always possible. Salvage yards do provide a great service by recycling historic building parts that might otherwise go to the landfill. If you're lucky, your local salvage yard will be indoors and highly organized. If you're not, it will be outdoors and you'll get to spend lots of time digging through soggy cardboard boxes in search of a piece of hardware.

HARDWARE STORES, HOME CENTERS, AND LUMBERYARDS

Old-fashioned hardware stores are indispensable. They will sell you the one washer you need to fix your faucet, may have all sorts of archaic hardware still in stock, and are rapidly becoming the last place that still sells slotted screws. They often employ people who have been around long enough to actually know something about old houses.

Home centers are certainly a fine place to buy joint compound, nails, plywood, thin set mortar, paint, and such. The lower prices may even balance out with the hassle of waiting in line, or the guilt of knowing they will eventually put the local hardware store and lumberyard out of business. Occasionally they even carry a few suitable light fixtures or sinks, and sometimes you can special-order something that would work. Other than basic supplies, however, few of them carry much that would be appropriate in a period bathroom.

A lumberyard is a must for real lumber, as home centers carry only the most basic sizes and woods. Real bead board, tongue-and-groove fir flooring, and 5/4 stock for cabinets will be found only at the lumberyard. Some lumberyards also have milling capacity and can make trim and molding to match what is already in the house. Some lumberyards are more like home centers and sell many other items besides lumber. There are also companies that specialize in moldings, flooring, or hardwoods, as well as companies that sell re-milled wood salvaged from old buildings.

CATALOGS AND WEBSITES

Almost any bathroom element can probably be ordered through the mail or over the Internet: fixtures, faucets, flooring, tile, wallpaper, hardware, cabinets, curtains, accessories, and more. Even plumbing fixtures from the legendary Thomas Crapper Company (still in business) are available on the Internet. This is especially useful for those living in areas where these kinds of items are not available locally. Back in the early part of the last century, the Sears Roebuck and Montgomery Ward catalogs served the same purpose. However, modern catalogs are printed on slick paper and thus are not useful to have a second life in the outhouse, as were their predecessors.

DOING IT YOURSELF

If you have the time and the skills (or are willing to learn the skills), doing it yourself will give you the most control over the end result. It can save you a great deal of money, depending, of course, on how many tools you have to buy or rent and how many times you screw up (and if you have to hire someone to fix what you screwed up). The problem with doing it yourself is that the learning curve can be quite steep, and once having learned to do something, you may never be called upon to do that thing again. You may want to do only parts of it yourself and hire out the rest. Doing it yourself requires patience, at least some aptitude, and a willingness to leap into the unknown. And it helps if you like doing this kind of stuff.

Particular jobs that lend themselves to doing yourself are those that are not difficult but are tedious and time-consuming, and, therefore, expensive to pay others to do. These include cleaning, paint stripping, wallpaper stripping, demolition, stripping paint from

Unable to match the stunning color of this purple tile, the home-owners opted to add white and black tile above the wainscoting when a shower was added to this tub. Installing simple ceramic tile is within the skills of intermediate do-it-yourselfers.

hardware, polishing hardware, taking stuff to the dump, and picking up needed supplies. (Why pay your contractor to stand in line at the lumberyard?) Other fairly easy tasks include paint prep, painting, patching small holes in plaster, and installing hardware, shelf coverings, and curtain rods. For those with more do-it-yourself experience, tasks such as installing ceramic tile, repairing wooden windows, laying linoleum or vinyl tile, installing light fixtures or faucets, and even hanging and taping drywall would be possible. Tasks for the really advanced might include running new wiring or plumbing, building an

The original bathroom in this 1908 plan-book bungalow was long gone when the current owners bought the house.
The newly installed bath, while containing all the modern conveniences—double sinks, separate medicine cabinets,
a low-flow toilet, capacious storage, and GFCIs—still has the same types of claw-foot tub, hexagonal-tile floor,
subway-tiled walls, and nickel-plated hardware and light fixtures that probably existed in the original bathroom.

addition, laying sheet flooring, building cabinets, or plastering. Many how-to books and magazines are devoted to all of these subjects.

It also helps to have the right tools. Some may be worth purchasing, depending on how often you are likely to use them. Some of the more expensive ones can be rented by the day or the week. Beyond the usual hammer, screwdrivers, wrenches, and pliers that most home tool kits should have, here are a few tools that are indispensable for restoration: a flat pry bar, a cat's-paw or nail puller, carbide paint scrapers, 5-in-1 tool, high-quality paintbrushes, locking pliers, reciprocating saw, jigsaw, power miter saw, belt sander, random orbit sander, table saw, power planer, circular saw, heat gun, drill, cordless drill, angle grinder, rotary tool, Roto-Zip, and the biggest, most powerful shop vacuum you can afford (get a Gore-Tex filter for it to deal with the plaster dust). Other specialized woodworking tools are needed for building cabinets, and a wet saw is a must for cutting ceramic tile. This is not an exhaustive list by any means, and the tools needed will depend on what you're going to be doing.

There is also the issue of time versus money. Doing it yourself will take longer. You may be better off spending that time at work earning the money to pay a contractor. Do you really want to spend all your spare time working on the bathroom? This is particularly an issue if there's only one bathroom. If there's no kitchen you can eat out, but how long can you really shower at the gym? Or go without a toilet? Be realistic about what you can do and how long it will take. Then halve what you think you can do and double the time it will take—this will be closer to reality.

And one other thing, learned from long experience: Don't do plumbing projects at night or on Sundays, because the plumbing supply place will be closed, and you will need the one part you can only get there.

CONCLUSION

The bathroom is the one room in the house that we use every single day, and the room most of us would not be willing to do without. It's the first place we use in the morning, and the last place we use before going to bed at night. We use it when we are ill, and we use it when we are healthy. We lock ourselves in the bathroom for privacy. Although we are not as reticent about it as the Victorians, we are still a little uncomfortable with the defecation aspect of bathrooms. You might install a bathtub or a sink in your bedroom, but it is unlikely you would install a toilet, even though, from an amount of usage standpoint, a toilet would make more sense.

Our obsession with cleanliness has reached heights never dreamed of by the sanitarians. Bathing and shampooing every day have become the norm, and some believe we are compromising our own immune systems by our increasing use of antibacterial cleansers. Nonetheless, improved sanitation may have far more to do with increased life expectancy in developed countries than any of the medical advances that are usually credited. Some believe that the best thing we could do for developing countries is to send them plumbers and help them build sewage systems.

Who knows what the future will bring? Perhaps by the end of this century we will be taking sonic showers like they do on *Star Trek* (although even in the *Star Trek* universe, a hot-water shower is considered luxurious). Considering the pace of change in twentieth-century bathrooms, I don't think there's any need to worry that a bungalow bathroom will become obsolete.

Resources

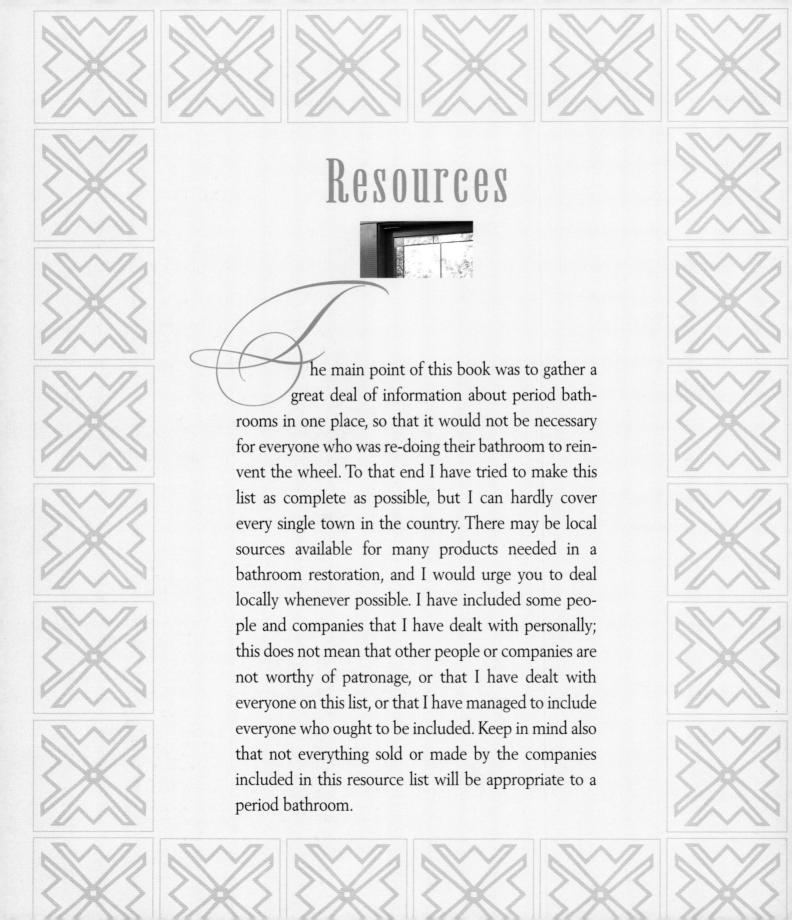

The main point of this book was to gather a great deal of information about period bathrooms in one place, so that it would not be necessary for everyone who was re-doing their bathroom to reinvent the wheel. To that end I have tried to make this list as complete as possible, but I can hardly cover every single town in the country. There may be local sources available for many products needed in a bathroom restoration, and I would urge you to deal locally whenever possible. I have included some people and companies that I have dealt with personally; this does not mean that other people or companies are not worthy of patronage, or that I have dealt with everyone on this list, or that I have managed to include everyone who ought to be included. Keep in mind also that not everything sold or made by the companies included in this resource list will be appropriate to a period bathroom.

CABINETRY

Steven Ballew
1521 37th St.
Sacramento, CA 95816
(916) 455-5908

Tim Brennan Co., Cabinetmakers
4 N. Oakwood Terr.
New Paltz, NY 12561
(914) 338-5757

**Marion H. Campbell,
Cabinetmaker**
39 Wall St.
Bethlehem, PA 18018
(610) 837-7775

Crown Point Cabinetry
153 Charlestown Rd.
Claremont, NH 03743
(800) 999-4994
www.crown-point.com

Cumberland Woodcraft Co.
10 Stover Dr./P.O. Drawer 609
Carlisle, PA 17013
(800) 367-1884
www.cumberlandwoodcraft.com

The Cutting Edge, Steven Crain
602A University Ave.
San Jose, CA 95110
(408) 276-1095
www.ceccabinets.com

Bill Eichenberger
580 Irwin St.
San Rafael, CA 94901
(415) 457-1190

Graham Lee Associates
Brian Krueger
2870 E. 54th St.
Vernon, CA 90058
(323) 581-8203

Kennebec Co.
1 Front St.
Bath, ME 04530
(207) 443-2131

Peter Kramer, Cabinetmaker
311 Gay St.
Washington, VA 22747
(540) 675-3625
www.peterkramer.com

Neil Kelly Cabinets
804 N. Alberta St.
Portland, OR 97217
(503) 335-9214
www.neilkelly.com

Christopher Peacock Cabinetry
151 Greenwich Ave.
Greenwich, CT 06830
(888) 609-9333

Plain and Fancy
Rt. 501 and Oak St.
Schaefferstown, PA 17088
(717) 949-6571

Plato Woodwork
200 Third St. SW/P.O. Box 98
Plato, MN 55370
(800) 328-5924

R and R Woodworks, Ron Reuter
P.O. Box 3084
Central Point, OR 97502
(541) 855-4428

Renaissance Cabinetmakers
PRI Box 2832
Arlington, VT 05250
(802) 375-9278

Restorations Unlimited
P.O. Box V/24 W. Main St.
Elizabethville, PA 17023
(717) 362-3477

**Ring Leg Furnishings/Full Design
Furniture, Bath and Kitchen**
134 Main St.
Gloucester, MA 01930
(508) 283-1039

Dana Robes, Wood Craftsman
Lower Shaker Village
P.O. Box 707
Enfield, NH 03748
(800) 722-5036
www.danarobes.com

Rutt Custom Cabinetry
P.O. Box 129/1564 Main St.
Goodville, PA 17528
(717) 445-3700
www.rutt1.com

Strasser and Associates
35 Hillside Ave.
Monsey, NY 10952
(914) 425-0650

Wellborn Cabinet
38669 Hwy.77/P.O. Box 1210
Ashland, AL 36251
(800) 762-4475

Wood Essentials
P.O. Box 843, Lenox Hill Station
New York, NY 10021
(212) 717-1112
www.woodessentials.com
(medicine cabinets)

Wood-Mode
(570) 374-2711
www.wood-mode.com

Yorktowne Cabinets
P.O. Box 231
Red Lion, PA 17356
(800) 777-0056
www.yorktowneinc.com

COUNTERTOPS
TILE

American Marazzi Tile
359 Clay Rd.
Sunnyvale, TX 75182
(972) 226-0110
www.am-marazzi.com

Amsterdam Corp.
150 E. 58th St.
New York, NY 10155
(212) 644-1350

Art Tile
4336 Broadway
Oakland, CA 94611
(510) 547-8288

B and W Tile Company
14600 South Western Ave.
Gardena, CA 90249
(310) 538-9579

Brooklyn Tile Supply Corp.
184 4th Ave.
Brooklyn, NY 11217
(718) 875-1789

California Clay
5427 Telegraph Ave., #Y
Oakland, CA 94609
(510) 655-1466
www.calclay.com

California Native Tile and Stone
1025 Carleton St., Studio 12
Berkeley, CA 94710
(510) 601-7565
www.tilest.com

California Pottery and Tile Works
859 E. 60th St.
Los Angeles, CA 90001
(323) 235-4151
www.MalibuTile.com

Classic Ceramic Tile
124 Tiles Ln.
East Brunswick, NJ 08816
(800) 394-7770
www.classiccerramictile.com

Country Floors
15 E. 16th St.
New York, NY 10003
(212) 627-8300

Creative Tile Marketing
222 SW 15th Rd.
Miami, FL 33129
(305) 858-8242

Daltile
7834 Hawn Fwy
P.O. Box 170130
Dallas, TX 75217
(800) 933-8453
www.daltile.com

Deer Creek Pottery
305 Richardson St.
Grass Valley, CA 95945
(530) 272-3373
www.aimnet.com/~tcolson/pages/
deercreek/dcpage.htm

Designs in Tile
Box 358-AB
Mt. Shasta, CA 96067
(530) 926-2629
www.designsintile.com

Endicott Clay Products
Box 17
Fairbury, NE 68352
(402) 729-3315

Epro, Inc.
156 E. Broadway
Westerville, OH 43081
(614) 882-6990

Esquire Ceramic Tile
300 International Blvd.
Clarksville, TN 37040
(800) 256-7924

Feature Tile
1001 Hidden Valley Rd.
Soquel, CA 95073
(831) 475-4602
www.featuretile.com

Firebird
335 Snyder Ave.
Berkeley Heights, NJ 07922
(908) 464-4613
www.firebirdtiles.com

Fireclay Tile
495 W. Julian St.
San Jose, CA 95110
(408) 275-1182
www.fireclay.com

Florida Tile Industries
P.O. Box 447
Lakeland, FL 33802
(941) 687-7171
www.fltile.com

Fulper Tile
34 W. Ferry St.
New Hope, PA 18938
(215) 862-3358

Handcraft Tile
1696 S. Main St.
Milpitas, CA 95035
(877) 262-1140
www.handcrafttile.com

Historical Hand Painted Tile
2104 E. Seventh Ave.
Tampa, FL 33605
(813) 247-6817

Marji Ingersoll, Tile Muralist
39040 S. Highway One
Gualala, CA 95445
(707) 884-4602
www.art.mcn.org/Marji-Ingersoll

Interceramic, USA
2333 S. Jupiter Rd.
Garland, TX 75041
(800) 496-8453
www.interceramicusa.com

London Tile Co.
65 Walnut St.
New London, OH 44851
(888) 757-1551
www.londontile.com

Malibu Ceramic Works
P.O. Box 1406
Topanga, CA 90290
(310) 455-2485

Marin DesignWorks
21-H Pamaron Dr.
Novato, CA 94949
(415) 884-2605
www.marindesignworks.com

William May and Co.
P.O. Box 234
Brielle, NJ 08730
(908) 528-2248

McIntyre Tile Co.
55 West Grant St.
Healdsburg, CA 95448
(707) 433-8866
www.mcintyre-tile.com

M. E. Tile Company
400 E. Sibley Blvd./P.O. Box 1595
Harvey, IL 60426
(708) 210-3229
www.metile.com

Mexican Handcrafted Tile/MC Designs
7595 Carroll Rd.
San Diego, CA 92121
(858) 689-9596

Mortarless Building Supply
2707-2719 Fletcher Dr.
Los Angeles, CA 90039
(323) 663-3291

Motawi Tileworks
33 N. Staebler, #2
Ann Arbor, MI 48103
(734) 213-0017
www.motawi.com

Native Tile and Ceramics
2317 Border Ave.
Torrance, CA 90501
(310) 533-8684

Pewabic Pottery
10125 East Jefferson Ave.
Detroit, MI 48214
(313) 822-0954
www.pewabic.com

Pratt and Larsen
1201 SE 3rd Ave.
Portland, OR 97214
(503) 231-9464

Red Clay Tile Works
75 Meade Ave.
Pittsburgh, PA 15202
(412) 734-2222

Renaissance Tile and Marble
P.O. Box 412
Cherry Valley, NY 13320
(607) 264-8474

Ann Sacks Tile and Stone
8120 NE 33rd
Portland, OR 97211
(503) 281-7751
www.annsacks.com

Seneca Tiles
7100 S. Country Rd., Ste 23
Attica, OH 44807
(800) 426-4335

Shep Brown Associates
24 Cummings Parkway
Woburn, MA 01801
(617) 935-8080

Summitville Tiles
P.O. Box 73
Summitville, OH 43962
(330) 223-1511

Terra Designs
24 East Blackwell St.
Dover, NJ 07801
(973) 328-1135

Terra Designs Tileworks
49B Rt. 202 S.
Far Hills, NJ 07931
(908) 234-0440

Terra Firma
16 Lotus Ln.
Aiken, SC 29801
(803) 643-9399

Tile Restoration Center
3511 Interlake Ave. N.
Seattle, WA 98103
(206) 633-4866

Tile Showcase
291 Arsenal St.
Watertown, MA 02172
(617) 926-1100

Urban Archaeology
143 Franklin St.
New York, NY 10013
(212) 431-4646

U.S. Ceramic Tile Co.
10233 Sandyville Rd. SE
East Sparta, OH 44626
(330) 866-5531
www.usceramictileco.com

Villeroy and Boch USA
(972) 488-2922
www.villeroy-boch.com

Wallech Art Tile
P.O. Box 4953
Sonora, CA 95370
(209) 928-4417

Waterworks
29 Park Ave.
Danbury, CT 06810
(800) 899-6757

Winters Tileworks
2547 Eighth St. #33
Berkeley, CA 94710
(510) 533-7624

STONE

Buckingham-Virginia Slate Corp.
P.O. Box 8
Arvonia, VA 23004
(804) 581-1131

Chiarini Marble and Stone
830 E. Washington Ave.
Santa Ana, CA 92701
(714) 547-5466

Echeguren Slate
1495 Illinois St.
San Francisco, CA 94107
(800) 992-0701
www.echeguren.com

Fireslate 2
(800) 523-5902
www.fireslate.com

Gawet Marble and Granite
Rt. 4 W/P.O. Box 219
Center Rutland, VT 05736
(802) 773-8868
www.vermontel.net/~gawet/

Renaissance Tile and Marble
P O Box 412
Cherry Valley, NY 13320
(607) 264-8474
www.tilemarbleandgranite.com

Ann Sacks Tile and Stone
(see Countertops - Tile)

Sheldon Slate Products
38 Farm Quarry Rd.
Monson, ME 04464
(207) 997-3615
www.sheldonslate.com

Shep Brown Associates
(see Countertops - Tile)

The Stone Yard
www.stoneyard.com

Structural Slate Co.
222 E. Main St./P.O. Box 187
Pen Argyl, PA 18072
(800) 677-5283
www.structuralslate.com

Tile Showcase
(see Countertops - Tile)

Vermont Soapstone
P.O. Box 268
248 Stoughton Pond Rd.
Perkinsville, VT 05151
(802) 263-5404

Vermont Structural Slate Co.
P.O. Box 98, 3 Prospect St.
Fair Haven, VT 05743
(800) 343-1900

Waterworks
(see Countertops - Tile)

WOOD

Aged Woods
2331 E. Market St.
York, PA 17402
(800) 233-9307
www.agedwoods.com

Albany Woodworks
(see Flooring - Wood)

Architectural Timber and Millwork
49 Mt. Warner Rd./P.O. Box 719
Hadley, MA 01035
(413) 586-3045

Augusta Lumber Co.
(see Flooring - Wood)

Authentic Pine Floors
(see Flooring - Wood)

Authentic Wood Floors
(see Flooring - Wood)

Barnes Lumber Mfg.
(see Flooring - Wood)

Carlisle Restoration Lumber
1676 Rt. 9
Stoddard, NH 03464
(800) 595-9663
www.wideplankflooring.com

Centre Mills Antique Floors
(see Flooring - Wood)

Chestnut Specialists
400 Harwinton Ave.
Plymouth, CT 06782
(860) 283-4209
www.chestnutspec.com

Chestnut Woodworking and Antique Flooring Co.
(see Flooring - Wood)

M.L. Condon Co.
(see Flooring - Wood)

Craftsman Lumber Co.
436 Main St.
Groton, MA 01450
(978) 448-5621
www.craftsmanlumber.com

Duluth Timber Co.
P.O. Box 16717
Duluth, MN 55816
(218) 727-2145
www.duluthtimber.com

Forester Moulding and Lumber
(see Flooring - Wood)

Goodwin Heart Pine Co.
(see Flooring - Wood)

Granville Mfg. Co.
(see Flooring - Wood)

The Joinery Co.
(see Flooring - Wood)

Longwood Restoration
330 Midland Pl., No. 3
Lexington, KY 40505
(800) 225-7857

Mountain Lumber Co.
P.O. Box 289
Ruckersville, VA 22968
(800) 445-2671
www.mountainlumber.com

New England Hardwood Supply
(see Flooring - Wood)

New England Wholesale Hardwoods
(see Flooring - Wood)

Patina Woods Co.
3563 New Franklin Rd.
Chambersburg, PA 17201
(717) 264-8009

Pioneer Millworks
1755 Pioneer Rd.
Shortsville, NY 14548
(800) 951-9663
www.newenergyworks.com/pmw

Plaza Hardwood
(see Flooring - Wood)

Quality Woods
63 Flanders Bartley Rd.
Lake Hiawatha, NJ 07034
(201) 584-7554

Rare Earth Hardwoods
(see Flooring - Wood)

River City Woodworks
825 Ninth St.
New Orleans, LA 70115
(800) 207-7738

A. E. Sampson and Son
(see Flooring - Wood)

Timberknee Ltd.
Waterman Rd.
South Royalton, VT 05068
(800) 720-9823

Timeless Wood
(see Flooring - Wood)

Woodhouse
(see Flooring - Wood)

The Woods Co.
(see Flooring - Wood)

World Class Floors
(see Flooring - Wood)

Yankee Exotic Woods
(see Flooring - Wood)

DECOR
ACCESSORIES

Art Deco Collection
546 Grand Ave.
Oakland, CA 94610
(510) 465-1920
www.artdecocollection.com

Fair Oak Workshops
P.O. Box 5578
River Forest, IL 60305
(800) 341-0597

Pottery Barn
P.O. Box 7044
San Francisco, CA 94120
(800) 922-5507
www.potterybarn.com

Curtains

Arts and Crafts Period Textiles
Dianne Ayres
5427 Telegraph W2
Oakland, CA 94609
(510) 654-1645

J. R. Burrows and Co.
P.O. Box 522
Rockland, MA 02370
(800) 347-1795
www.burrows.com

Country Curtains
Red Lion Inn, Main St.
Stockbridge, MA 01262
(800) 456-0321
www.countrycurtains.com

Earth Runnings
P.O. Box 3027
Taos, NM 87571
(505) 758-5703
www.earthrunnings.com

Especially Lace
202 Fifth St.
West Des Moines, IA 50265
(515) 277-8778

Liberty Valances and Curtains
768 N. Fairoaks Ave.
Pasadena, CA 91103
(626) 395-9997
www.libertyvalances.com

London Lace
215 Newbury St.
Boston, MA 02116
(800) 926-5223
www.londonlace.com

Prairie Textiles
Ann Wallace and Friends
P.O. Box 2344
Venice, CA 90244
(213) 617-3310
www.webmonger.com/AnnWallace

Rue de France
78 Thames St.
Newport, RI 02940
(401) 846-2084
www.ruedeFrance.com

Charles Rupert
2005 Oak Bay Ave.
Victoria, BC V8R 1E5
Canada
(250) 592-4916
www.charles-rupert.com

Thistle Handwerks
P. O. Box 21578
Billings, MT 59104
(416) 896-9434
www.thistlehandwerks.com

United Crafts
127 West Putnam Ave. #123
Greenwich, CT 06830
(203) 869-4898

Vintage Valances
Box 43326
Cincinnati, OH 45243
(513) 561-8665

Stencils

Helen Foster Stencils
71 Main St.
Sanford, ME 04073
(207) 490-2625

Trimbelle River Studios
Amy A. Miller
P.O. Box 568
Ellsworth, WI 54011
(715) 273-4844
www.trimbelleriver.com

Designers

Artistic License
P.O. Box 881841
San Francisco, CA 94188
(415) 675-9996
(crafts guild)

Denise Hice
4812 West Washington Blvd.
Milwaukee, WI 53208
(414) 476-8023
(interior design)

Karen Hovde, Interior Vision
23 Oakshore Ct.
Port Townsend, WA 98368
(888) 385-3161
(interior design)

Susan Mooring Hollis
Historic Interiors
77 Lexington Rd.
Concord, MA 01742
(508) 371-2622

Ivy Hill Interiors
Laurie Taylor
3920 SW 109th St.
Seattle, WA 98146
(206) 243-6768
(interior design)

National Kitchen and Bath Association
(800) 843-6522
www.nkba.org
(referrals to Certified Kitchen and Bath Designers)

Victorian Interiors
575 Hayes St.
San Francisco, CA 94102
(415) 431-7191
(interior design)

Marti Wachtel
1376 Yosemite Ave.
San Jose, CA 95126
(408) 998-2545
(interior design)

Electrical

Classic Accents
P.O. Box 1181
Southgate, MI 48195
(313) 941-8011
(push-button light switches)

Fixtures, Faucets, Plumbing

A-Ball Plumbing Supply
1703 W. Burnside
Portland, OR 97209
(800) 228-0134
www.a-ball.com

Affordable Antique Bath and More
P.O. Box 444/333 Oak St.
San Andreas, CA 95249
(888) 303-2284
www.bathandmore.com

American Standard
One Centennial Ave.
Piscataway, NJ 08855
(800) 524-9797
www.americanstandard.com

Antique Baths and Kitchens
2220 Carlton Way
Santa Barbara, CA 93109
(805) 962-2598

Antique Hardware and Home
19 Buckingham Plantation Dr.
Bluffton, SC 29910
(800) 422-9982

Barclay Products
4000 Porett Dr.
Gurnee, IL 60031
(847) 244-1234

Bathroom Machineries
P.O. Box 1020/495 Main St.
Murphys, CA 95247
(800) 255-4426
www.deabath.com

Baths From The Past
83 E. Water St.
Rockland, MA 02370
(800) 697-3871
www.bathsfromthepast.com

Brasstech
3131 Standard Ave.
Santa Ana, CA 92705
(714) 436-0805
www.brasstech.com

Burgess Intl. Bath Fixtures
6810 Metroplex
Romulus, MI 48174
(800) 837-0092
www.parliamentplumbing.com

Cheviot Products
200-1594 Kebet Way
Port Coquitlam, BC V3C 5M5
Canada
(800) 444-5969
www.cheviotproducts.com

Chicago Faucets
2100 S. Clearwater Dr.
Des Plaines, IL 60018
(847) 803-5000

The Copper Sink Co.
P.O. Box 732
Los Olivos, CA 93441
(805) 693-0733

Country Plumbing
5042 Seventh St.
Carpinteria, CA 93013
(805) 684-8685

Crane Plumbing
1235 Hartrey Ave.
Evanston, IL 60202
(847) 864-9777
www.craneplumbing.com

Creme de la Creme
131 Sunrise Ave., Unit #1
Toronto, ON M4A 1B2
Canada
(877) 701-1021
www.cremedelacremeglobal.com

Delta Faucet
55 E. 11th St.
Indianapolis, IN 46280
(800) 345-3358
www.deltafaucet.com

Dick's Antiques
670 Lake Ave.
Bristol, CT 06010
(860) 584-2566

**Do It UR Self Plumbing and
Heating Supply**
3100 Brighton Blvd.
Denver, CO 80216
(303) 297-0455

Doors of London
10903 Terrace Dr.
Forestville, CA 95436
(707) 887-1879
www.doorsoflondon.com

Eljer Plumbingware
17120 Dallas Pkwy.
Dallas, TX 75248
(972) 407-2600
www.eljer.com

Gemini Bath and Kitchen Products
P.O. Box 43398
Tucson, AZ 85733
(520) 770-0667
www.geminibkp.com

George's Plumbing
690 S. Fairoaks Ave.
Pasadena, CA 91106
(626) 792-5547

**GNU Plumbing and Hardware
Restoration**
999 Pennsylvania Ave.
Monaca, PA 15061
(724) 728-5955

Harrington Brass Works
7 Pearl Ct.
Allendale, NJ 07401
(201) 818-1300
www.harringtonbrassworks.com

J. B. Products
500 Oakdale Rd.
Lake Zurich, IL 60047
(847) 438-4141

Johnson and Johnson Antiques
6820 Greenwood Ave. N.
Seattle, WA 98103
(206) 789-6489

Kohler
444 Highland Dr.
Kohler, WI 53044
(414) 457-4441
www.kohlerco.com

Kolson
653 Middle Neck Rd.
Great Neck, NY 11023
(516) 487-1224
www.kolson.com

Mac the Antique Plumber
6325 Elvas Ave.
Sacramento, CA 95819
(800) 916-2284

Mansfield Plumbing Products
8425 Pulsar Pl.
Columbus, OH 43240
(614) 825-0960
www.mansfieldplumbing.com

Opella
4062 Kingston Ct.
Marietta, GA 30060
(800) 969-0339

The Renovator's Supply
P.O. Box 2515
Conway, NH 03818
(800) 659-2211

Restoration Works
812 Main St.
Buffalo, NY 14202
(716) 856-6400
www.restoworks.com

Rohl LLC
1559 Sunland Ln.
Costa Mesa, CA 92626
(714) 557-1933

St. Thomas Creations
1022 West 24th St., Ste. 125
National City, CA 91950
(800) 536-2284
www.stthomascreation.com

The Sink Factory
2140 San Pablo Ave.
Berkeley, CA 94702
(510) 540-8193
www.sinkfactory.com

**Strom Plumbing by Sign of the
Crab**
3756 Omec Cr.
Rancho Cordova, CA 95742
(800) 843-2722
www.signofthecrab.com

Sunflower Shower Head Company
P.O. Box 4218
Seattle, WA 98104
(206) 722-1232
www.deweyusa.com/deweyusa

Sunrise Specialty Co.
930 98th Ave.
Oakland, CA 94603
(800) 646-9117
www.sunrisespecialty.com

George Taylor Specialties
100 Hudson St., Store B
New York, NY 10013
(212) 226-5369

Thomas Crapper and Co. Ltd.
The Stable Yard, Alscot Park
Stratford-on-Avon, Warwickshire,
UK
Phone: 01789-450-522
thomas-crapper.co.uk

Tile-Redi
2570 N. Powerline Rd.,
Ste. 504
Pompano Beach, FL 33069
(888) 445-TILE
www.tileredi.com
(pre-fabricated shower pans)

Toto USA
1155 Southern Rd.
Morro, GA 30260
(800) 350-8686
www.totousa.com

Touch of Brass
9052 Chevolet Dr.
Ellicott City, MD 21042
(800) 272-7734
www.atouchofbrass.com

Ultra Baths
956 Chemin Olivier
St. Nicolas, PQ G7A 2N1
Canada
(800) 463-2187
www.ultrabaths.com

Vintage Plumbing
9645 Sylvia Ave.
Northridge, CA 91324
(818) 772-1721
www.vintageplumbing.com

Watercolors
Garrison, NY 10524
(914) 424-3327

Watermark
491 Wortman Ave.
Spring Creek, NY 11208
(800) 842-7277

Watertown Supply Company
33 Grove St.
Watertown, MA 02472
(800) 323-3233
www.watertownsupply.com
(Custom-sized shower curtains.)

Waterworks
(see Countertops - Tile)

Woodmark International/Banner Faucets
216 North Interurban
Richardson, TX 75081
(800) 346-8435

FIXTURE REFINISHING

Miracle Method
4239 North Nevada, Ste. 115
Colorado Springs, CO 80907
(800) 444-8827
www.miraclemethodusa.com

Perma Ceram Enterprises
65 Smithtown Blvd.
Smithtown, NY 11787
(800) 645-5039

Perma-Glaze
1638 S. Research Loop Rd., #160
Tucson, AZ 85710
(800) 332-7397
www.permaglaze.com

Porcelain Industries
215 Union Blvd.
West Islip, NY 11795
(516) 661-4023
www.porcelainindustries.com

FLOORING
LINOLEUM

Laurie Crogan
10386 Tupelo Ln.
Los Angeles, CA 90077
(310) 474-1821
(custom designed floors)

Forbo Industries
(800) 342-0604
www.forbo-industries.com

Linoleum City
5657 Santa Monica Blvd.
Hollywood, CA 90038
(323) 469-0063

TILE

(see Countertops - Tile)

WOOD

Albany Woodworks
P.O. Box 729
Albany, LA 70711
(504) 567-1155
www.albanywoodworks.com

Augusta Lumber Co.
567 N. Charlotte Ave.
Waynesboro, VA 22980
(540) 946-2841
www.comclin.net/augustalumber

Authentic Pine Floors
P.O. Box 206/4042 Hwy. 42
Locust Grove, GA 30248
(800) 283-6038

Authentic Wood Floors
P.O. Box 153
Glen Rock, PA 17327
(717) 428-0904

Barnes Lumber Mfg.
P.O. Box 1383
Statesboro, GA 30459
(912) 764-8875
www.barneslumber.com

Centre Mills Antique Floors
P.O. Box 16
Aspers, PA 17304
(717) 334-0249
www.igateway.com/mall/home
imp/wood/index

Chestnut Woodworking and Antique Flooring Co.
P.O. Box 204
West Cornwall, CT 06796
(860) 672-4300

M. L. Condon Co.
254 Ferris Ave.
White Plains, NY 10603
(914) 946-4111

Forester Moulding and Lumber
152 Hamilton St.
Leominster, MA 01453
(800) 649-9734
www.forestermoulding.com

Goodwin Heart Pine Co.
106 SW 109th Pl.
Micanopy, FL 32667
(352) 466-0339
www.heartpine.com

Granville Mfg. Co.
Rt. 100/P.O. Box 15
Granville, VT 05747
(802) 767-4747
www.woodsiding.com

The Joinery Co.
P.O. Box 518
Tarboro, NC 27886
(919) 823-3306

Launstein Hardwoods
384 S. Every Rd.
Mason, MI 48854

Linden Lumber
P.O. Drawer 480369/Hwy. 43N
Linden, AL 36748
(334) 295-8751

Mayse Woodworking Co.
319 Richardson Rd.
Lansdale, PA 19446
(888) LONGLEAF

Millwork Designs
230 Topaz Ln.
Washington C.H., OH 43160
(740) 335-5203

New England Hardwood Supply
100 Taylor St.
Littleton, MA 01460
(800) 540-8683

New England Wholesale Hardwoods
Rt. 82 S.
Pine Plains, NY 12567
(518) 398-9663
www.floorings.com

Plaza Hardwood
5 Enebro Ct.
Santa Fe, NM 87505
(505) 438-3260

J. L. Powell and Co.
600 S. Madison St.
Whiteville, NC 28472
(800) 227-2007

Rare Earth Hardwoods
6778 E. Traverse Hwy.
Traverse City, MI 49684
(800) 968-0074

Robbins Flooring
25 Whitney Dr., Ste. 106
Milford, OH 45150
(800) 733-3309
www.robbinsflooring.com

A. E. Sampson and Son
P.O. Box 1010/171 Camden Rd.
Warren, ME 04864
(207) 273-4000

Simmen Wholesale Lumber
7641 Wilbur Way, Ste. A
Sacramento, CA 95828
(916) 689-9112

Timeless Wood
RR 1, Box 49A
Irasburg, VT 05845
(888) 515-0886

Vintage Pine Co.
P.O. Box 85
Prospect, VA 23960
(804) 574-6531

Woodhouse
P.O. Box 7336
Rocky Mount, NC 27804
(919) 977-7336

The Woods Co.
610B Fifth Ave.
Chambersburg, PA 17201
(717) 263-6524

World Class Floors
333 SE Second Ave.
Portland, OR 97214
(800) 547-6634
www.contactintl.com

Yankee Exotic Woods
P.O. Box 211
Cornish, NH 03746
(603) 675-6206

HISTORIC BED AND BREAKFASTS

Manka's Inverness Lodge
P.O. Box 1110
Inverness, CA 94937
(415) 669-1034

Warfield House
318 Buffalo St.
Elkins, WV 26241
www.bbonline.com/wv/warfield

GLASS

S. A. Bendheim Co.
61 Willett St.
Passaic, NJ 07055
(800) 221-7379
(restoration glass)

Blenko Glass Co.
P.O. Box 67/Fairgrounds Rd.
Milton, WV 25541
(304) 743-9081
www.citynet.net/blenko

Glashaus
450 E. Congress Parkway, Ste. E
Crystal Lake, IL 60014
(815) 356-8440
www.glashaus.com

Glass Block Designs
P.O. Box 410594
San Francisco, CA 94141
(415) 626-5770
www.glassblockdesigns.com

Glasslight
P.O. Box 310
St. Peters, PA 19470
(610) 469-9066

Pittsburgh Corning Corporation
800 Presque Isle Dr.
Pittsburgh, PA 15239
(800) 624-2120
www.pittsburghcorning.com

HARDWARE

Acorn Mfg.
457 School St., Box 31
Mansfield, MA 02048
(800) 835-0121
www.acornmfg.com

Addkison Hardware Co.
126 E. Amite St.
P.O. Box 102
Jackson, MS 39205
(800) 821-2750
www.addkisonhardware.com

Affordable Antique Bath and More
(see Fixtures)

Al Bar-Wilmette Platers
127 Green Bay Rd.
Wilmette, IL 60091
(847) 251-0187
(hardware restoration)

American Home Supply
191 Lost Lake Ln.
Campbell, CA 95008
(408) 246-1962

Antique Doorknob
Publishing Co.
P.O. Box 2609
Woodinville, WA 98072
(425) 483-5848
(books about hardware, research
archive)

Antique Hardware and Home
(see Fixtures)

Architects and Heroes Interiors
1809 W. 35th St.
Austin, TX 78703
www.knobshop.com

Ball and Ball
463 W. Lincoln Hwy.
Exton, PA 19341
(610) 363-7330

Bathroom Machineries
(see Fixtures)

Bauerware Cabinet Hardware
3886 17th St.
San Francisco, CA 94114
(415) 864-3886
www.bauerware.com

Bona Decorative Hardware
3073 Madison Rd.
Cincinnati, OH 45209
(513) 321-7877

Brainerd Manufacturing Co.
115 N. Washington St.
East Rochester, NY 14445
(716) 586-0028

Brass Menagerie
524 St. Louis
New Orleans, LA 70130
(504) 524-0921

The Broadway Collection
1010 W. Santa Fe/P.O. Box 1210
Olathe, KS 66051
(913) 782-6244

Canaan Distributors
20 Largo Park
Stamford, CT 06907
(800) 882-6226

A Carolina Craftsman
975 S. Avocado St.
Anaheim, CA 92805
(714) 776-7877

Cirecast
380 Seventh St.
San Francisco, CA 94103
(415) 863-8319

Crown City Hardware Co.
1047 N. Allen Ave.
Pasadena, CA 91104
(626) 794-1188
www.crowncityhardware.com

Decorative Hardware Studio
P.O. Box 627
Chappaqua, NY 10514
(914) 238-5251
www.decorative-hardware.com

Elliot's Hardware Plus
P.O. Box 36027
Dallas, TX 75235
(888) 638-8963
www.oldtyme.com

Emtek
15250 E. Stafford
City of Industry, CA 91744
(800) 356-2741
www.emtekproducts.com

Englewood Hardware Co.
25 N. Dean St.
Englewood, NJ 07631
(201) 568-1937

Eugenia's Antique Hardware
5370 Peachtree Rd.
Chamblee, GA 30341
(800) 337-1677

Franklin Brass
P.O. Box 4887
Carson, CA 90749
(310) 885-3200
www.franklinbrass.com

Garbe Industries
4137 S. 72nd East Ave.
Tulsa, OK 74145
(800) 735-2241
www.garbes.com

Grandpa Snazzy's Hardware
1832 S. Broadway
Denver, CO 80210
(303) 778-6508

Grant Co.
349 Peel St.
New Hamburg, ON N0B 2G0
Canada
(519) 662-3892

Hardware Bath and More
20830 Coolidge Hwy.
Oak Park, MI 48237
(248) 398-4560
www.h-b-m.com

Hinges and Handles
P.O. Box 103
100 Lincolnway E.
Osceola, IN 46561
(219) 674-8878

Horton Brasses
Nooks Hill Rd.
Cromwell, CT 06416
(860) 635-4400
www.horton-brasses.com

Imperial Decorative Hardware
1429 W. Collins
Orange, CA 92867
(714) 288-6022

Kayne and Son Custom Hardware
100 Daniel Ridge Rd.
Candler, NC 28715
(828) 667-8868

Kolson
(see Fixtures)

Kraft Hardware
306 E. 61st St.
New York, NY 10021

Lenape Products
600 Plum St.
Trenton, NJ 08638
(609) 394-5376
www.lenapebath.com

Liz's Antique Hardware
453 S. La Brea
Los Angeles, CA 90036
(323) 939-4403
www.lahardware.com

Mac the Antique Plumber
(see Fixtures)

Nostalgic Warehouse
701 E. Kingsley Rd.
Garland, TX 75041
(800) 522-7336
www.nostalgicwarehouse.com

Paxton Hardware
P.O. Box 256
Upper Falls, MD 21156
(800) 241-9741
www.paxtonhardware.com

Period Brass
31-35 Water St.
Jamestown, NY 14701
(800) 332-6677

Phelps Company
60 Elm St.
Brattleborough, VT 05301
(802) 257-4314

Plexicraft Products
5406 San Fernando Rd.
Glendale, CA 91203
(818) 246-8201
www.plexicraft.com

The Renovator's Supply
(see Fixtures)

Restoration Works
(see Fixtures)

Simon's Hardware/Bath
421 Third Ave.
New York, NY 10016
(212) 532-9220
www.simons-hardware.com

Touch of Brass
(see Fixtures)

Upper Canada Specialty Hardware
10 Brent Cliffe Rd., Unit 14
Toronto, ON M4G 3Y2
Canada
(877) 877-7232
www.ucsh.com

Valli and Valli
150 E. 58th St., 4th Fl.
New York, NY 10155
(877) 326-2565
www.vallievalli.com

Van Dyke's Restorers
Fourth Ave. and Sixth St.
Woonsocket, SD 57385
(800) 558-1234
www.vandykes.com

Victoria Specialty Hardware
1976 Oak Bay Ave.
Victoria BC V8R 1E2
Canada
(888) 274-6779

Woodworker's Store
4365 Willow Dr.
Medina, MN 55340
(612) 478-8201
www.woodworkerstore.com

Heating

Easy Heat
31977 U.S. 20
New Carlisle, IN 46552
(800) 537-4732
www.easyheat.com

Enerjee
24 S. Lafayette Ave.
Morrisville, PA 19067
(215) 295-0557
www.enerjee.com

Heatway
3131 W. Chestnut Expwy.
Springfield, MO 65802
(800) 255-1996
www.heatway.com

Infloor Heating Systems
P.O. Box 253
920 Hamel Rd.
Hamel, MN 55340
(800) 588-4470
www.infloor.com

Myson
49 Hercules Dr., Ste. 4904
Colchester, VT 05446
(800) 698-9690
www.mysoninc.com

Northern Wholesale Supply
6800 Otter Lake Rd.
Lino Lakes, MN 55038
(800) 666-1111

Radiant Electric Heat
3695 N. 126th St., Unit N
Brookfield, WI 53005
(800) 774-4450
www.electricheat.com

Reggio Register Company
P.O. Box 511
Ayer, MA 01432
(978) 772-3493
www.reggioregister.com

WarmlyYours.com
965 Ponderosa Ln.
Barrington, IL 60010
(800) 875-5285
www.warmlyyours.com

House Museums and Historic Sites

The Adamson House
23200 Pacific Coast Hwy.
Malibu, CA 90265
(310) 456-8432

Ardenwood Historic Farm
Patterson House
34600 Ardenwood Blvd.
Fremont, CA 94555
(510) 796-0663

The Biltmore Estate
One North Pack Sq.
Asheville, NC 28801
(800) 543-2961

Craftsman Farms
2353 Rt. 10 W.
Morris Plains, NJ 07950
(973) 540-1165
www.parsippany.net/
craftsmanfarms.html

Dearborn House
Historic Seattle
1117 Minor Ave.
Seattle, WA 98101
(206) 622-6952

Dunsmuir House
2960 Peralta Oaks Ct.
Oakland, CA 94605
(510) 615-5555

**The Frank Lloyd Wright Home
and Studio**
951 Chicago Ave.
Oak Park, IL 60302
(708) 848-1500
www.wrightplus.org

The Gamble House
4 Westmoreland Pl.
Pasadena, CA 91103
(626) 793-3334

The Glessner House
1800 S. Prairie Ave.
Chicago, IL 60616
(312) 922-3432

**President Warren G. Harding
Home**
380 Mt. Vernon Ave.
Marion, OH 43302
(800) BUCKEYE

Heritage Hill Historic Park
Bennett Ranch House
25151 Serrano Rd.
Lake Forest, CA 92630
(949) 855-2028

Idaho State Historical Museum
610 N. Julia Davis Dr.
Boise, ID 83072
(208) 334-2120

The Lanterman House
4420 Encinas Ave.
La Cañada-Flintridge, CA 91012
(818) 790-1421

Living History Farms
2600 NW 11th St.
Urbandale, IA 50322
(515) 278-5286

The Marston House
3215 Seventh Ave.
San Diego, CA 92103
(619) 232-2654

The Rev. McKinney House
8369 University Ave.
La Mesa, CA 91941
(619) 466-0197

The Pleasant Home
217 S. Home Ave.
Oak Park, IL 60302
(708) 383-2654

The Purcell-Cutts House
2328 Lake Pl.
Minneapolis, MN 55405
(612) 870-3133

Riordan House
409 Riordan Rd.
Flagstaff, AZ 86001
(520) 779-4395

The Stimson-Green Mansion
1204 Minor Ave.
Seattle, WA 98101
(206) 624-0475
(private building—available
for events)

Harriet Beecher Stowe House
77 Forest St.
Hartford, CT 06105
(203) 522-9258

Strong Museum
One Manhattan Square
Rochester, NY 14607
(716) 263-2700

LIGHTING

Aamsco Lighting
15-17 Brook St.
Jersey City, NJ 07302
(800) 221-9092
www.aamsco.com
(reproduction Edison bulbs)

American Home Supply
(see Hardware)

Antique Lighting Co.
1000 Lenora St., Ste. 314
Seattle, WA 98121
(206) 622-8298

Ball and Ball
(see Hardware)

Bathroom Machineries
(see Fixtures)

Joan Bogart Antiques
Box 265
Rockville, Center, NY 11571
(516) 764-5712

Brass Light Gallery
131 S. First St.
Milwaukee, WI 53204
(800) 243-9595
www.brasslight.com

Brass 'N Bounty
68 Front St.
Marblehead, MA 01945
(781) 631-3864

Brass Reproductions
9711 Canoga Ave.
Chatsworth, CA 91311
(818) 709-7844

**Brooke Grove Antique and Custom
Lighting**
21412 Laytonsville Rd.
Laytonsville, MD 20882
(301) 948-0392

City Lights
2226 Massachsetts Ave.
Cambridge, MA 02140
(617) 547-1490

Classic Illumination
2743 Ninth St.
Berkeley, CA 94710
(510) 849-1842

Ensler Lighting
1793 Solano Ave.
Berkeley, CA 94707
(510) 526-4385

Gaslight Time
5 Plaza St. W.
Brooklyn, NY 11217
(718) 789-7185

Historic Lighting
10341 Jewell Lake Ct.
Fenton, MI 48430
(810) 629-4934

Historic Lighting
114 East Lemon Ave.
Monrovia, CA 91016
(626) 303-4899
www.historiclighting.com

Howard's Antique Lighting
203 Hillsdale Rd./Rt. 23
South Egremont, MA 01258
(413) 528-1232
(restoration)

Kruesel's General Merchandise
22 Third St. S.W.
Rochester, MN 55902
(507) 289-8049

Kyp-Go
526 Geneva Rd.
Glen Ellyn, IL 60137
(630) 942-8181
(reproduction Edison bulbs)

Light Power
59A Wareham St.
Boston, MA 02118
(617) 423-9790
www.genuineantiquelighting.com

Liz's Antique Hardware
(see Hardware)

**Metropolitan Lighting
Fixture Co.**
200 Lexington Ave.,
Showroom 512
New York, NY 10016
(800) 233-4500

Meyda Tiffany
1 Meyda Fine Pl.,
55 Oriskany Blvd.
Yorkville, NY 13495
(800) 222-4009

Neri Antiques
313 South St.
Philadelphia, PA 19147
(215) 923-6669

Newstamp Lighting Co.
P.O. Box 189/227 Bay Rd.
North Easton, MA 02356
(508) 238-7071

Nick's Fabrication
550 Vandalia St.
St. Paul, MN 55114
(612) 646-8395

Nowell's
490 Gate 5 Rd./P.O. Box 295
Sausalito, CA 94966
(415) 332-4933

The Original Cast Lighting
6120 Dellmar Blvd.
St. Louis, MO 63112
(314) 863-1895
www.theOCL.com

Pennsylvania Globe Gaslight Co.
300 Shaw Rd.
North Branford, CT 06471
(203) 484-7749
www.pennglobe.com

Progress Lighting
P.O. Box 5704
Spartanburg, SC 29304
(864) 599-6000

Fredrick Ramond
16121 South Carmenita Rd.
Cerritos, CA 90703
(562) 926-1361

Rejuvenation Lamp and Fixture Co.
2550 NW Nicolai St.
Portland, OR 97210
(888) 343-8548
www.rejuvenation.com

Restoration Works
(see Fixtures)

Riverwalk Lighting and Gifts
401 South Main St.
Naperville, IL 60540
(630) 357-0200

Roy Electric Co.
22 Elm St.
Westfield, NJ 07090
(800) 366-3347
www.westfieldnj.com/roy

Ruiz Antique Lighting
2333 Clement Ave.
Alameda, CA 94501
(510) 769-6082

St. Louis Antique Lighting Co.
801 N. Skinker Blvd.
St. Louis, MO 63130
(314) 863-1414

Things Deco
130 E. 18th St., Ste. 8F
New York, NY 10003
(212) 362-8961

Turn of the Century Lighting
112 Sherbourne St.
Toronto, ON M5A 2R2
Canada
(416) 362-6203

Urban Archaeology
(see Countertops)

Victorian Lighting, Inc.
29 York St.
Kennebunk, ME 04043
(207) 985-6868

Victorian Lighting Works
P.O. Box 469
Centre Hall, PA 16828
(814) 364-9577

Victorian Revival
356 Richmond Rd.
Ottawa, ON K2A 0E8
Canada
(613) 722-1510

Organizations

American Association for State and Local History
1717 Church St.
Nashville, TN 37203
(615) 320-3203
www.aaslh.org

Friends of Terra Cotta
771 West End Ave., Ste. 10E
New York, NY 10025
(212) 932-1750
www.preserve.org

National Terrazzo and Mosaic Association
110 E. Market St., Ste. 200A
Leesburg, VA 20176
(800) 323-9736

National Trust for Historic Preservation
1785 Massachusetts Ave. NW
Washington, DC 20036
(202) 588-6000
www.nationaltrust.org

Tile Heritage Foundation
P.O. Box 1850
Healdsburg, CA 95448
(707) 431-TILE

The Victorian Society in America
219 S. Sixth St.
Philadelphia, PA 19106
(215) 627-4252
www.libertynet.org/~vicsoc

Periodicals

American Bungalow
123 S. Baldwin Ave.
Sierra Madre, CA 91024
(800) 350-3363
www.ambungalow.com

**Fine Homebuilding
Fine Woodworking**
The Taunton Press
63 S. Main St./P.O. Box 5506
Newtown, CT 06470
(203) 426-8171
www.finehomebuilding.com

Old House Interiors
2 Main St.
Gloucester, MA 01930
(978) 283-3200
www.oldhouseinteriors.com

Old House Journal
1 Thomas Cr. NW, Ste. 600
Washington, DC 20005
(202) 729-3500
www.oldhousejournal.com

Restoration Consultants

Steven Ballew
1521 37th St.
Sacramento, CA 95816
(916) 455-5908

Benriter Restoration
John Benriter
2300 Stonyvale Rd.
Tujunga, CA 91042
(818) 353-1136

Paul Duchscherer
303 Roosevelt Way
San Francisco, CA 94114
(415) 861-6256
pduchscherer@earthlink.net

House Dressing
Jane Powell
P.O. Box 31683
Oakland, CA 94604
www.bungalowkitchens.com
hsedressng@aol.com

Restoration True
Norman Finnance
P.O. Box 90367
San Jose, CA 95109
(408) 910-6970
nfinnance@earthlink.net

Salvage Yards

Adkins Architectural Antiques
3515 Fannin St.
Houston, TX 77004
(713) 522-6547

American Salvage
9200 NW 27th Ave.
7001 NW 27th Ave.
Miami, FL 33147
(305) 691-7001
www.americansalvage.com

Architectural Accents
2711 Piedmont Rd.
Atlanta, GA 30305
(404) 266-8700

Architectural Antique and Salvage
Co. of Santa Barbara
726 Anacapa St.
Santa Barbara, CA 93101
(805) 905-2446

Architectural Antiques
801 Washington Ave. N.
Minneapolis, MN 55401
(612) 332-8344

Architectural Antiques Exchange
715 N. Second St.
Philadelphia, PA 19123
(215) 922-3669

Architectural Antiquities
Harborside, ME 04642
(207) 326-4938

Architectural Artifacts
2207 Carimer St.
Denver, CO 80033
(303) 292-6812

Architectural Artifacts
4325 N. Ravenswood Ave.
Chicago, IL 60613
(773) 348-0622

Architectural Elements
818 E. Eighth St.
Sioux Falls, SD 57103
(605) 339-9646

Architectural Elements
503 150th St.
Amery, WI 54001
(605) 339-9646

Architectural Emporium
207 Adams Ave.
Canonsburg, PA 15317
(724) 222-8586

Architectural Salvage
1215 Delaware St.
Denver, CO 80204
(303) 615-5432

Architectural Salvage
103 W. Michigan
201 E. Michigan
Grass Lake, MI 49240
(517) 522-8715

Architectural Salvage Warehouse
212 Battery St.
Burlington, VT 05401
(802) 658-5011
www.architecturalsalvagevt.com

Architectural Salvage, W. D.
618 E. Broadway
Louisville, KY 40202
(502) 589-0670

Architectural Warehouse of Historic
York
224 N. George St.
York, PA 17401
(717) 854-7152

Artefacts Architectural Antiques
P.O. Box 513
St. Jacobs, ON N0B 2N0
Canada
(519) 664-3760
www.artefactsaa.com

Bauer Bros.
2500 Elm St.
Minneapolis, MN 55414
(612) 331-9492

Berkeley Architectural Salvage
1167 65th St.
Oakland, CA 95608
(510) 655-2270

Bill's Architectural Antiques
600 W. 131st St.
New York, NY 10027
(212) 281-0916

The Brass Knob
2311 18th St. NW
Washington, DC 20009
(202) 332-3370
www.washingtonpost.com/yp/
brassknob

By-Gone Days Antiques
3100 South Blvd.
Charlotte, NC 28209
(704) 527-8717

Colonial Antiques
5000 W. 96th St.
Indianapolis, IN 46268
(317) 873-2727

Dick's Antiques
670 Lake Ave.
Bristol, CT 06010
(860) 584-2566

Governor's Antiques and
Architectural Materials
8000 Antique Ln.
Mechanicsville, VA 23116
(804) 746-1030

Great Gatsby's
5070 Peachtree Industrial Blvd.
Atlanta, GA 30341
(800) 428-7297

Johnson and Johnson Antiques
6820 Greenwood Ave. N.
Seattle, WA 98103
(206) 789-6489

Kimberly's Old-House Gallery
1600 Jonquill Ln.
Wausau, WI 54401
(715) 359-5077

Materials Unlimited
2 W. Michigan Ave.
Ypsilanti, MI 48197
(800) 299-9462
www.mat-unl.com

Morrow's
2784-B Jacksonville Hwy.
Medford, OR 97501
(541) 770-6867

Myers Restoration and
Architectural Salvage
RFD 2, Box 1250
Clinton, ME 04927
(207) 453-7010

Off the Wall, Architectural
Antiques
P.O. Box 4561
Lincoln near Fifth
Carmel, CA 93921
(408) 624-6165
www.imperialearth.com/OTW/

Ohmega Salvage
2407 San Pablo Ave.
Berkeley, CA 94702
(510) 843-7368

Old Home Supply
1801 College Ave.
Fort Worth, TX 76110
(817) 927-800

The Old House Parts Co.
24 Blue Wave Mall
Kennebunk, ME 04043
(207) 985-1999
www.oldhouseparts.com

Olde Good Things
124 W. 24th St.
New York, NY 10011
(212) 989-8401
www.oldegoodthings.com

Olde Theatre Architectural
Salvage Co.
2045 Broadway
Kansas City, MO 64108
(816) 283-3740

Brad Oliver Antiques
Box 303
Cresco, PA 18326
(717) 595-3443

Omega Too
2204 San Pablo Ave.
Berkeley, CA 94702
(510) 843-3636

Osceola Antiques
117 Cascade St.
Osceola, WI 54020
(715) 294-2886

Pinch of the Past
109 W. Broughton St.
Savannah, GA 31401
(912) 232-5563

Salvage Heaven
6633 W. National Ave.
West Allis, WI 53214
(414) 329-7170
www.salvageheaven.com

Salvage One
1524 Sangamon St.
Chicago, IL 60608
(312) 733-0098
www.salvageone.com

Scavenger's Paradise
5453 Satsuma Ave.
North Hollywood, CA 91601
(323) 877-7945

Seattle Building Salvage
330 Westlake Ave. N.
Seattle, WA 98109
(206) 381-3453

Shank and Nickell Kitchen and
Bath Works
736 Walnut St.
Royersford, PA 19468
(610) 948-9200

Soll's Antiques
P.O. Box 307
Canaan, ME 04924
(207) 474-5396
www.somtel.com/solantiq

This and That
1701 Rumrill Blvd.
San Pablo, CA 94806
(510) 232-1273

United House Wrecking
535 Hope St.
Stamford, CT 06906
(203) 348-5371
www.united-antiques.com

Urban Archaeology
(see Countertops)

Vermont Salvage Exchange
P.O. Box 453
White River Junction, VT 05001
(802) 295-7616

VENTILATION

Broan/Nu-Tone Group
926 W. State St.
Hartford, WI 53027
(800) 558-1711
www.broan-nutone.com

Fantech
1712 Northgate Blvd.
Sarasota, FL 34234
(800) 747-1762
www.fantech-us.com

WALLS

Charles St. Supply Co.
54 Charles St.
Boston, MA 02114
(800) 382-4360
(plaster washers)

Fastenation
P.O. Box 520068
Winthrop, MA 02152
(617) 846-6444
(plaster washers)

WALLPAPER

Bradbury and Bradbury
P.O. Box 155
Benicia, CA 94510
(707) 746-1900
www.bradbury.com

Carter and Co./Mt. Diablo
Handprints
451 Ryder St.
Vallejo, CA 94590
(707) 554-2682

Crown Corp., NA
2485 W. Second Ave.
Denver, CO 80223
(800) 422-2099

Eisenhart Wallcoverings
P.O. Box 464
Hanover, PA 17331
(800) 931-WALL
www.eisenhartwallcoverings.com

Fairman/Peerless Wallpaper
and Blinds
1411 Fifth Ave.
Pittsburgh, PA 15219
(412) 471-6955
www.wallpaperguide.com/
peerless

Imperial Home Decor Group
23645 Mercantile Rd.
Cleveland, OH 44122
(800) 539-5399
www.ihdg.com

Victorian Collectibles
845 East Glenbrook Rd.
Milwaukee, WI 53217
(800) 783-3829
www.victorianwallpaper.com

WEBSITES

Craftsman Home Connection
www.crafthome.com

The Faucet Doctor
www.thefaucetdoctor.net

www.heatinghelp.com

www.lightsearch.com

Outhouses of America Tour
www.jldr.com/ohindex.shtml

www.paintedpotties.com
(toilet and sink basin decals)

Plumbing and Mechanical
Magazine
PMMag.com

PlumbingStore.com

PlumbingWorld.com
RestorationCentral
www.restorationcentral.com

www.vintagetub.com

wallpaperguide.com

WebWilson.com
www.webwilson.com

World of Feng Shui
www.wofs.com

WINDOWS AND DOORS

Allegheny Restoration
P.O. Box 18032
Morgantown, WV 26507
(304) 594-2570
www.mountain.net/ha/
allegheny-restoration

Andersen Corp.
100 4th Ave.
Bayport, MN 55003
(800) 426-4261
www.andersenwindows.com

Architectural Components
26 N. Leverett Rd.
Montague, MA 01351
(413) 367-9441

Architectural Detail in Wood
41 Parker Rd.
Shirley, MA 01464
(978) 425-9026

Artistic Doors and Windows
10 S. Inman Ave.
Avenel, NJ 07001
(908) 726-9400

J. S. Benson Woodworking and
Design Co.
26 Birge St.
Brattleboro, VT 05301
(802) 254-3515

Bristolite Skylights
401 E. Goetz Ave./P.O. Box 2515
Santa Ana, CA 92707
(800) 854-8618
www.bristolite.com

Marion H. Campbell
(see Cabinetry)

Charles River Restoration
P.O. Box 390
Hopkinton, MA 01748
(508) 435-8540
(copper frame skylights)

Colorado House of Doors
6976 County Rd. 107
Salida, CO 81201
(719) 539-4568

Combination Door Company
1000 Morris St./P.O. Box 1076
Fond du Lac, WI 54936
(414) 922-2050

Copper Beech Millwork
30 Industrial Dr.
Northhampton, MA 01061
(800) 532-9110
www.copperbeech.com

CountryPlank.com
P.O. Box 415
Lisbon, MD 21765
(410) 489-2526
www.countryplank.com

Crestline Windows and Doors
888 Southview Dr.
Mosinee, WI 54455
(715) 693-7000
www.crestlineonline.com

Dad's Woodshop
19475 St. Clair Ave.
Cleveland, OH 44117
(216) 383-8808

Drums Sash and Door Co.
P.O. Box 207
Drums, PA 18222
(717) 788-1145

Eagle Window and Door
375 E. Ninth St.
Dubuque, IA 52004
(319) 556-2270
www.eaglewindow.com

Englander Millwork Corp.
2369-71 Lorillard Pl.
Bronx, NY 10458
(718) 364-4240

Eton Architectural Millwork
1210 Morse Ave.
Royal Oak, MI 48067
(248) 543-9100

Feather River Door
2345 Forest Ave.
Chico, CA 95928
(800) 395-3667
www.featherdoor.com

Fine Woodworking Co.
16750 White Store Rd.
Boyds, MD 20841
(301) 972-8808

H. Hobein and Son
160 Snelson Rd.
Marshall, NC 28753
(828) 649-3238

Holtzer and Fenestra LLC
233 Butler St.
Brooklyn, NY 11217
(718) 254-0858

Hornspier Millwork
1690 S. Lake Michigan Dr.
Sturgeon Bay, WI 54235
(920) 743-8823

Kolbe and Kolbe Millwork
1323 S. 11th Ave.
Wausau, WI 54401
(800) 955-8177
www.kolbe-kolbe.com

Lititz Planing Mill
302 E. Front St.
Lititz, PA 17543
(717) 626-2186

Littleton Millwork
44 Lafayette Ave.
Littleton, NH 03561
(603) 444-2677

Malta Windows
P.O. Box 397, 13th St.
Malta, OH 43758
(740) 962-3131
www.maltawindows.com

**Midwest Architectural Wood
Products**
300 Trails Rd.
Eldridge, IA 52748
(319) 285-8000

Millwork Supply Co.
2225 First Ave. S.
Seattle, WA 98134
(206) 622-1450

Morgan Mfg.
P.O. Box 2446
Oshkosh, WI 54903
(414) 235-7170

J. P. Moriarty Millwork
22 Clifton St.
Somerville, MA 02144
(617) 628-3000

**Oakwood Classic and Custom
Woodworks, Ltd.**
517 W. Commercial St.
East Rochester, NY 14445
(716) 381-6009
www.oakwoodww.com

Peachtree Doors and Windows
4350 Peachtree Industrial Blvd.
Norcrosss, GA 30071
(800) PEACH99
www.peach99.com

Pella Corp.
102 Main St.
Pella, IA 50219
(800) 84PELLA
www.pella.com

Pozzi Windows
P.O. Box 5249
Bend, OR 97708
(800) 537-6880
www.pozzi.com

Rails and Stiles
145 Cherokee Trail
Indian Springs, AL 35124
(205) 967-2662

Restoration Supply Co.
736 Walnut St.
Royersford, PA 19468
(610) 948-9200

Ricketson Sash and Door
100 Bidwell Rd.
South Windsor, CT 06074
(860) 289-1222

Seekircher Steel Window Repair
2 Weaver St.
Scarsdale, NY 10583
(914) 725-1904
www.atsrc.com/dessite/
seekirch.htm

Semco
P.O. Box 378
Merrill, WI 54452
(800) 333-2206
www.semcowindows.com

H. Syder and Company
640 East Fairchild St.
Danville, IL 61832
(217) 446-8443

**Zeluck Architectural Wood
Windows and Doors**
5300 Kings Hwy.
Brooklyn, NY 11234
(800) 233-0101

Make him [the reader] laugh and he will think you a trivial fellow, but bore him in the right way and your reputation is assured.

—W. Somerset Maugham

BIBLIOGRAPHY

Beecher, Catherine, and Harriet Beecher Stowe. *American Woman's Home.* New York: J. B. Ford and Co., 1869. Reprint: New Brunswick, New Jersey: Rutgers University Press, 1998.

Clow and Donaldson. *Standard American Plumbing: Hot Air, Hot Water Heating, Steam and Gas Fitting.* Chicago: Frederick J. Drake & Co., 1911.

Croutier, Alev Lytle. *Taking The Waters.* New York: Abbeville Publishing Group, 1992.

Hart-Davis, Adam. *Thunder, Flush, and Thomas Crapper.* London: Michael O'Mara Books, 1997.

Horan, Julie L. *The Porcelain God: A Social History of the Toilet.* Secaucus, New Jersey: Carol Publishing, 1997.

Jester, Thomas C. *Twentieth Century Building Materials.* Washington, DC: McGraw-Hill Companies, 1995.

Lambdon, Lucinda. *Temples of Convenience and Chambers of Delight.* London: Pavilion Books, 1998.

Lupton, Ellen, and J. Abbott Miller. *The Bathroom, the Kitchen and the Aesthetics of Waste: A Process of Elimination.* New York: Princeton Architectural Press, 1992.

Maddock, Thomas. *Pottery.* Trenton, New Jersey: Thomas Maddock's Sons' Company, 1910.

National Trust for Historic Preservation. *The Well-Appointed Bath.* Washington, DC: The Preservation Press, 1989.

Ogle, Maureen. *All the Modern Conveniences.* Baltimore, Maryland: The Johns-Hopkins University Press, 1996.

Pathak, Bindeswar, Ph.D, Litt. D. *History of Public Toilets.* Paper presented at the International Symposium on Public Toilets.

Prentice, Blair, Helaine Kaplan, and the City of Oakland Planning Department. *Rehab Right.* Oakland, California: City of Oakland, 1978. Reprint, Berkeley, California: Ten Speed Press, 1986.

_____. *Sears Roebuck and Co. Consumer's Guide Fall 1909.* 1909. Reprint, New York: Ventura Books, 1979.

_____. The Editors of Sunset Books and Sunset Magazine. *Sunset Bathrooms Planning and Remodeling.* Menlo Park, California: Lane Publishing Co., 1983.

_____. *The Victorian Bathroom Catalogue.* London: Random House, 1996.

Wilson, Henry L. *A Short Sketch of the Evolution of the Bungalow: From its Primitive Crudeness to its Present State of Artistic Beauty and Cozy Convenience.* Los Angeles, n.d. Reprint as *California Bungalows of the Twenties.* Mineola, New York: Dover Publications, 1993.

_____. *Building with Assurance.* Chicago: Morgan, 1921. Reprint as *Homes and Interiors of the 1920s: A Restoration Design Guide.* New York: Sterling Publishing, 1987.

Wright, Lawrence. *Clean and Decent: The Fascinating History of the Bathroom and the W.C.* London: Routledge & Kegan Paul, Ltd., 1960. Reprint, London: Book Club Associates, 1971.